The Batsford Book of

HOME FURNISHINGS

By the same author and published by Batsford:
Lampshades: Technique and Design
The Batsford Book of Soft Furnishings

The Batsford Book of

HOME FURNISHINGS

Angela Fishburn

B T Batsford Ltd, London

To my husband

First published 1982
© Angela Fishburn 1982

ISBN 0 7134 3466 X

Printed in Great Britain by the Anchor Press Ltd
Tiptree, Essex
for the publishers, B T Batsford Ltd,
4 Fitzhardinge Street, London W1A 0AH

CONTENTS

INTRODUCTION

Making soft furnishings for the home has become a popular occupation in recent years. Because of the high cost of having these made professionally, Do-It-Yourself has become a necessity for most homemakers, and it has become essential to have a working knowledge of this important craft.

It is not difficult to develop a flair for decorating and furnishing your home if a study has been made of the basic principles of colour and design. The ability to interpret ideas is a challenge. However, those with a good working knowledge of soft-furnishing techniques should be able to achieve a professional decorator's finish as well. I hope that this book will serve as a complete guide in this direction and fire the imagination and enthusiasm of beginners as well as of those with previous experience. I hope that you will enjoy using the ideas I have suggested, but I also hope that the techniques in this book will give you the confidence and the ability to try out your own designs, and in those too to achieve a truly professional finish.

Acknowledgment

I would like to thank Jackie Allen for the line illustrations, and Katie Beckett for her help in reading the transcript.

The black and white photographs came from the following sources. Laura Ashley (9); Crown Wallcoverings (10); Descamps (1, 4 and 7); Pallu and Lake (6 and 8); Rufflette (2) and Tissunique (3 and 5). Colour photographs 2, 3 and 4 were supplied by Laura Ashley, and 1 by Pallu and Lake. The jacket photographs were from Laura Ashley.

1

COLOUR AND DESIGN IN THE HOME

Homes need to be dressed, rather as people do, and it is often necessary to disguise some architectural shortcomings and to develop or exaggerate others. Developing a decorating scheme and making the soft furnishings and accessories — experimenting with colour, texture and fabrics to discover harmony or contrast — can bring a great sense of achievement when the final picture unfolds.

When furnishing a home it is important to remember that it is not only the loose covers and curtains that are necessary to achieve a good visual effect, but all the small accessories such as padded hangers, table napkins, personalised pillowcases, interesting pelmets, etc. These smaller items all add up to the very special place that we call home, where we should be comfortable and happy. Our homes reflect our personalities, like the clothes we wear. Home should be a relaxing place in which to live and entertain our families and friends. A successful decorating scheme, therefore, is one that is constantly giving us pleasure, confidence and satisfaction.

Try to achieve the maximum effect with the least expense. Remember that costly fabrics do not necessarily provide the most interesting schemes. Look at the less expensive fabrics and see how, with a little imagination, they can be used to advantage. Try to develop a decorator's flair by using unexpected materials to create exciting effects.

Colour, design and texture are the three considerations to be taken into account when making a successful decorating scheme. In order to understand how these three work together it is important to study each separately before attempting to combine them.

The Oxford Dictionary defines colour as 'the sensation produced in the eye of rays of decomposed light.' Colour, therefore is only present when there is light. The colour of something seen in sunlight is different from that seen in candlelight because the intensity of the light being reflected from the object's surface is different, and the colour appears to vary. Colour is also influenced by its surroundings, and can take an entirely fresh tone when accompanied by different colours or textures.

The colour wheel is the starting point in planning a decorative scheme. It is often called nature's rainbow. Make a simple colour wheel and see how it works. Experiment with paper and paint. Notice how the wheel is divided into two — one half providing the warm colours (reds, oranges and yellows) and the other half providing the cool colours (greens, blues and purples) (*fig. 1*).

The Principles of Colour

Primary colours: There are three primary colours — red, yellow and blue. These are the three basic constituents of the colour spectrum.

Secondary colours: These colours are produced by mixing two adjoining primary colours together — orange (made by mixing red and yellow), green (made by mixing blue and yellow) and purple (made by mixing blue and red). An infinite number of colours can be

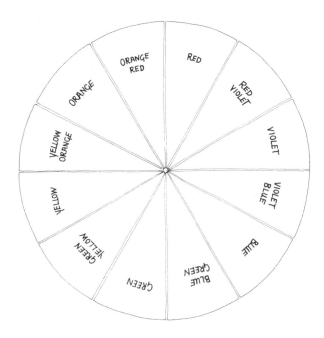

Fig. 1 *The colour wheel*

obtained by mixing secondary colours in varying proportions.

Neutrals: In addition to the primary and secondary colours there are two neutrals — black and white. White reflects the light and absorbs other colours around it. Black absorbs the light and intensifies the colours around it and so makes things look brighter. Black and white are of course the extremes of the neutrals, but there are also greys and browns. These vary considerably and can create warmth or coolness. A grey/blue, for example, would be cooler than a grey/yellow. This also applies to browns, an orange/brown being warmer than a blue/brown.

Hue: A hue is a colour in its purest form.

Tone: Tone is the darkening or lightening of these pure colours.

Colour value: This is the ability of a colour to reflect light.

Harmony: The colours that are adjacent to each other in the colour circle are known to be in harmony with each other; for example, green, blue/green, blue.

Complementary: Complementary colours lie opposite to one another in the colour circle and are in contrast to each other. The main complementaries are red and green, yellow and violet, and orange and blue. But colours between these still have their complementary colour directly opposite on the wheel and there can be many subtle gradations if wished.

Discordant: These are colours that are out of their natural order and are conflicting. They are neither in harmony, nor complementary to each other. They do not therefore coexist well and can create an inharmonious combination.

Points to Bear in Mind when Using Colour

(1) Try to understand as much as possible about colour and how it works (see Bibliography). Use it with confidence and flair and do not be afraid of it.

(2) A colour (or hue) is influenced by the one that adjoins it, and it appears lighter or darker depending on that influence. Experiment with colours, putting one against the other and giving them different backgrounds. Notice how the colours change when doing this. Use paper and paint or scraps of fabric and see how many different effects can be achieved.

(3) Look at wallpapers, fabrics, etc. both in daylight and in artificial light.

(4) The tone of the colours (the degree of lightness and darkness) changes with the gradual movement of the sun throughout the day. Therefore a room and its furnishings will appear different with the variations in intensity of light from dawn to dusk each day. It will also be affected by the amount and type of artificial light produced by lamps and bulbs.

(5) Colour creates illusions of shape and size — hence the ability to make a room look larger or smaller, narrower or wider. Remember too, that a colour appears brighter when used in large areas.

Design

The size, shape and layout of a room should be complemented and enhanced by the patterns and visual shapes created by the fabrics. Much can be achieved by bearing in mind the following points:

(1) Train the eye to appreciate good design. Look carefully at film and television sets, glossy magazines and window displays. Much can be learnt by studying the work of professional designers in many fields and noting how pattern and shape are used.

(2) Too much pattern in the same room is ineffective, although today's trend is towards using many patterns with a common theme or in subtle harmony. Pattern must be used skilfully, taking balance and contrast into account.

(3) Horizontal or diagonal stripes can be used to advantage, as can trellis designs. These work well with some patterned fabrics and papers.

(4) Use small or geometric patterns in small rooms and keep larger patterns for use in large areas. Very large patterns are usually more suited to public buildings and hotels. It is important to keep patterns in proportion to the room size.

(5) As well as being decorative, any furnishing fabric chosen should suit its purpose and be truly functional.

Texture

Texture adds yet another dimension to the decorating scheme. Take into account the floor area — whether woodblock, tiled or carpeted. Brick walls, fireplaces and polished furniture must also be taken into consideration for the texture and colour they provide. Texture can add interest to a room without the need for colour. Natural surfaces, such as wood, brick, rush matting or knobbly tweed can be the perfect background for a successful scheme.

Contrast in texture is as important as contrast in colour. Texture affects the value of colour. For example, a coloured article which has a rough, textured object placed next to it will look quite different when placed beside a smooth, shiny-surfaced one. This is because the shiny object reflects the light but the rough object absorbs it. Variations in texture give interest to a room, so experiment by collecting as many fabrics as possible in the same colour but in different textures.

Planning an Interior Design

To make a successful decorating scheme it is necessary to look at the picture as a whole and not be tempted to consider each item in isolation. The professional interior decorator looks at his work dispassionately and decides on the treatment he will use, for logical reasons. He then chooses fabrics and accessories which will work well together, and the result is usually a pleasing visual effect.

The home decorator will want to create a scheme that suits both the aspect of the room and its purpose, and also — very importantly — that she/he will not tire of quickly. So first choose the basic or main colour, and then work round it.

There are three types of scheme that work well:

Monochromatic: This is a scheme using different tones and amounts of one colour. This can be most effective if care is given to balance and pattern, and interest created by variations in texture. Too much of the same tone can be boring, so use a few bright accessories.

Related: This uses colours that are adjoining on the colour wheel. Use of these related colours creates a restful, harmonious scheme (e.g. blues/greens).

Contrasting: A contrasting, or complementary, scheme is one which uses two colours that are opposite to one another on the colour wheel. It is often advisable, however, to let one colour dominate, as this creates a more interesting scheme, and then to use a vibrant colour to give emphasis to a particular focal point (e.g. yellow/violet).

Ideas for Planning

(1) Make a sketch of the room noting electrical points, elevations and existing furniture. Collect samples of fabrics, wallpapers and paints. Keep a folder for each room scheme and take it along when shopping for samples.

(2) Consider the aspect of the room. North and east-facing rooms demand warm colour schemes to counteract the lack of sunshine and low intensity of light. Base the scheme on the warmer tones of the colour wheel — reds, oranges or yellows. Rooms that face south and west may have strong sunlight streaming in during the day. They can take the cool fresh colours of blues and greens.

(3) Decide on a basic colour which is pleasing to those who use the room most. Ideally the floor covering should be chosen first, the wall colour next and then the curtains or blinds. These usually represent the three largest areas of colour and texture in the room and will therefore have the most impact. They must work well together.

(4) If planning from scratch, consider having the same basic floor colour throughout the house, or certainly make sure that adjoining floor coverings are in harmony with each other. This creates a great sense of spaciousness and continuity, and enables room schemes to be built around a common colour. Separate schemes must, of course, be made for each room, but by using varying amounts of colour, texture and pattern, a very pleasing, balanced visual effect can be achieved. Take particular care when choosing floor coverings; they should make a harmonious background for many colours.

(5) Collect samples of fabrics suitable for the main items of soft furnishings, e.g. curtains, loose covers and upholstery. Use complementary colours for the smaller accessories such as cushions, table linen, lampshades, tissue boxes, etc.

(6) Remember that by grouping accessories together — whether cushions, ornaments or plants — you give them more impact.

(7) Do not always play safe and create a monochromatic scheme. Create impact by adding startling touches of contrasting or complementary colours. For example, when using yellow as a basic colour, accessory colours could be orange, pink or bright green.

(8) Distribute the colours around the room so that the overall effect satisfies the eye. Too much pattern on one side of the room creates an unbalanced effect. Experiment by placing furniture in different positions to give emphasis to a particular feature. If possible, group seating so as to take advantage of any sunlight.

(9) Try to create an integrated colour scheme for the whole house or unit. It is not always possible to do this all at once, but can be achieved gradually over a number of years. Remember that rooms often open out onto another and by carrying the colours through and linking them skilfully together a much more restful scheme is achieved throughout the house. Colours can be linked by the choice of a basic floor covering colour. If a patterned wallpaper is used in one room, have a plain or textured wall covering in the room that adjoins it. Pick out a colour from the wallpaper in one room and work round it to create a pleasing scheme for the next, using variations in texture and amounts of colour. In this way the eye will not be confused with too many colours and the finished scheme will be restful and balanced.

(10) Keep abreast of current trends in furnishing fashions, ideas and accessories — but only follow them if they happen to satisfy your particular need.

(11) Keep a scrapbook, and collect cuttings of ideas and colour schemes that have a special appeal and show furnishing flair.

(12) In decorating and furnishing, pale colours recede, deep colours appear to be closer, hence the possibility of making a room look larger and smaller, narrower and wider. Dark colours give a warmer effect than light ones. Light colours create spaciousness and make a room look larger and lighter. To create an illusion of space, avoid large-patterned fabrics for walls and furnishings and also large pieces of furniture. Keep patterns and furniture in scale with the size of the room.

(13) Draw the eye to important features in the room by using dominant colours, pattern or design. For example, make a bold, interestingly shaped pelmet to draw the eye away from a difficult window, or choose a plain textured lampshade to draw attention to an ornate base.

(14) Chair covers or bedcovers can provide the main contrast to the basic colour chosen. They should tone or contrast well in colour, texture and pattern.

(15) Do not be tempted to copy any room setting precisely. Let it rather be a source of inspiration for your own ideas.

Visits to stately homes and historic houses can be great sources of inspiration both for design and colour.

(16) A change is as good as a rest. It is not always possible to make major changes to a room, but consider the possibility of replacing cushions or lampshades in different colours or styles. Think about accessories and how they can alter a room — new pillowcases and sheets can give a bedroom a new lease of life. A different tablecloth and matching lampshade will give fresh interest in the kitchen or dining room. Furnishing on a budget is indeed a challenge, but there are many good decorative ideas that are inexpensive and simple to adapt to individual needs.

(17) The same basic principles apply when furnishing the garden as when furnishing the house. Though we cannot change the colour of the sky or grass, we can re-paper a ceiling or wall, so when making tablecloths or cushions for the garden aim for an effect that will be visually pleasing and which will not detract from the natural beauty of the garden or terrace. Furnishings in the garden should enhance and not compete with nature, so beware of fabrics with patterns or large bunches of artificial looking flowers. Choose, instead, geometric patterns, stripes, checks or plains. Use piping and other decorative finishes to add impact to the finished scheme.

2
FABRICS AND THEIR CARE

The history and development of textiles over the years is a vast and fascinating subject, and for those interested in more detailed study several comprehensive books have been written (see Bibliography). It is necessary to have a sufficient knowledge of fabrics and their origin and content, and it is important to know something of their different properties and behaviour and to be able to assess their suitability for their use in soft furnishings and accessories for the home.

Fabrics fall into two categories — natural and man-made. Natural fibres are based on raw materials from animal and vegetable sources; man-made fibres are those manufactured by chemically treating raw materials such as minerals and vegetables.

Natural fibres
Silk: Silk is the fine thread which is reeled from the cocoon of the silkworm larva, then wound on bobbins to be woven into fabric. It is manufactured mainly in the East, although France has long been renowned as the centre of silk manufacture in Europe. Silk is expensive to produce as the insects which spin the fibres are costly to rear. It has great strength but is weakened by strong sunlight. Its use now has been largely replaced by that of man-made fibres, such as rayon, as these, using vegetable cellulose, are much quicker and cheaper to produce. Silk is, therefore, a luxury fabric and is little used in soft furnishings, except for lampshades, cushions and other small accessories. It dyes extremely well and many subtle colours can be obtained. It is

crease resistant, washes well, and has a natural lustre which many other fabrics lack.
Wool: Woollen thread is produced from the twisted strands of hair shorn from the bodies of sheep, the alpaca and some species of goat. The fibres of sheep's wool vary in length and thickness according to the breed. The coarser fibres are used for carpets and rugs; the finer fibres are made into furnishing fabrics, and are often blended with other fibres to give a crease-resistant quality. Wool is soft, warm and, being virtually uncrushable, a good choice for upholstery fabrics and carpets. Wool dyes well and can be rendered shrink-resistant, water-repellent, stain-repellent and mothproof. It is sometimes machine-washable.
Cotton: The cotton plant is a flowering shrub whose yellow blooms become covered with tufts of cotton wool. This is picked, carded and spun to produce cotton thread and fabric. Cotton is economic to produce, and all the fibres can be used, so there is little wastage. Strong and hard-wearing, it washes well, and can be easily printed and dyed. Cotton fabric can be treated with several finishes and can be rendered shrink-resistant, crease-resistant, stain-repellent, drip-dry, minimum iron, flameproof and water-repellent. It can also be glazed, which renders the fabric dirt-resistant, and can be treated with special insulating properties which make it suitable for lining curtains. It is a versatile fabric and is often blended with other fibres. It is a very suitable choice for many items of home furnishings.
Linen: Linen is a textile fabric woven from the fibres produced by the flax plant, which is

14

cultivated in Northern Ireland, the Netherlands, Belgium, Russia and New Zealand. It is particularly hardwearing and does not shrink, but in its natural form creases easily. It is often blended with other fibres to give furnishing fabrics added strength. Linen has a smooth texture and does not hold the dirt. It washes easily and is stronger wet than dry, but the fibres are weakened if exposed to strong sunlight. Linen can be rendered crease-resistant, and it is particularly suitable for making loose covers because of its strength and wearing properties. It is extensively used for making tablecloths and table napkins and, in the form of buckram, for making firm lampshades.

Man-made fibres

Great developments have recently taken place in the manufacture of man-made fibres, and progress is constantly being made in this field. New processes and techniques are being introduced to improve the properties of the fabrics, and it is often very difficult to distinguish them from the natural fibres which they imitate.

Man-made fibres are produced by chemically treating basic raw materials such as wood pulp, petroleum extracts, by-products of coal, casein, cotton linters and groundnuts. Most of the fabrics produced are not absorbent, and tend to look dirty rather quickly. This is because the dirt stays on the surface and is not absorbed by the fabric. However, this makes it easy to clean. Most synthetic fibres can be blended with natural fibres or other man-made fibres to produce fabrics with varying uses and finishes, strengths and resilience.

Viscose rayon: This was the first synthetic fibre to be produced in Britain, at the end of the last century. Its basic raw material is wood pulp. It is very versatile and has the appearance of silk, and was originally known as artificial silk. It is easy to wash and can be rendered crease-resistant, flame-resistant and water repellent.

Acetate rayon: This is also manufactured from wood pulp, but it is not so versatile and hard-wearing as viscose rayon. More care is needed during washing and it will melt if subjected to high temperatures. Special flame-resistant types of acetate are produced for use in furnishing fabrics. It has good draping qualities. It is weaker when wet and when exposed to strong sunlight. It absorbs moisture readily and so is likely to shrink.

P.V.C. (Polyvinyl chloride): This is strong, has a shiny surface and is resistant to many chemicals. It can be easily wiped clean or washed by hand in warm water and is often used for outdoor furnishings, tablecloths, aprons, and so on. It is very sensitive to heat and cannot be ironed.

Acrylics: These are fibres made from coal and oil and will withstand strong sunlight. Acrylics have a high resistance to abrasion yet they remain soft to the touch. They wash well and do not shrink or stretch, and are therefore particularly good for soft furnishing fabrics. The fibres can be spun in many ways to simulate different fabrics made from natural fibres.

Choice of Fabrics for Furnishings and Accessories

Some fabrics used for soft furnishings

Polyester cotton sheeting: This fabric, made partly from natural cotton fibres and partly from man-made fibres, comes in widths suitable for making into single and double sheets as well as duvet covers and pillow cases. It is useful for making valances, curtains, and can be used for covering small tables. It washes well, needs little ironing, and is very versatile because it is made in co-ordinating plain colours and prints.

Tentcloth and deckchair canvas: These are firm, closely woven fabrics made from 100% cotton and are suitable for making sag bags and floor cushions and also for covering garden furniture.

Downproof cambric: This is a firm, closely woven cotton fabric which is specially waxed on one side to prevent the down working through the fabric. The waxed side should be placed next to the filling in order to be effective. It is used for making duvets that are to be filled with down of any kind, and also for making cushion pads and pillows.

Unbleached calico: This is strong cotton fabric used extensively in soft furnishings. It is comparatively inexpensive and very hard-wearing.

Bump: A thick, soft, fluffy fabric made of cotton waste, it is obtainable bleached or unbleached and is usually 122 cm (48 in) wide. It is used for interlining curtains and pelmets and is a good insulator. It can also be used for quilting. It cannot be washed and must only be dry cleaned.

Domette: This is similar to bump but not quite so thick and fluffy, and has the same uses.

Pelmet buckram: Pelmet buckram is golden brown in colour and is made from coarse canvas impregnated with glue. It is sold by the meter and is usually in narrow widths of 45.5 cm (18 in). It is used for making curtain tie-backs as well as pelmets.

Buckram: This is obtainable by the metre and varies in depth from 7.5 cm (3 in) to 15 cm (6 in). It is used for stiffening hand-made curtain headings, and can be ironed on to the fabric, using a steam iron.

Synthetic wadding: This is available in various widths, weights and thicknesses and has many uses in the home. Synthetic wadding is completely washable and non-absorbent, and is therefore a useful filling for cushions, duvets, quilts and pillows.

Ticking: This is available in plain white, or in black and white stripes. It is used for making pillows and cushions, and is usually 140 cm (54 in) wide.

When choosing and buying furnishing fabrics there are many points to remember:

(1) Buy the best quality fabric you can afford. This may not necessarily be the most expensive, but it should be the one that offers the best value for money.

(2) Buy furnishing fabrics for soft furnishing. This is what they are made for. Dress materials can sometimes be used for smaller accessories, but they are not so durable, and as they are made in narrower widths, extra care must be taken to check the requirements needed.

(3) Look at the manufacturer's label to see what claims are made. Is it shrink-resistant, fade-resistant, drip-dry, crease-resistant? If possible visit the manufacturer's showrooms to see the fabrics displayed to advantage. The staff are trained to help and advise on the selection available, and this can be very useful when important decisions on choice of fabrics have to be made.

(4) Make sure that the fabric suits the purpose for which it is intended and that it is practical to maintain.

(5) When making loose covers choose a fabric that will resist dirt well and that will not crease. It is important to choose a closely woven fabric that is hard-wearing and washable.

(6) Curtain fabric should drape well and be fade-resistant; ask to see the material draped both to check its draping qualities and to see the effect that light has on the fabric from the back and the front.

(7) There are many patterned fabrics of good design. Choose a well-known manufacturer and select fabrics that are printed correctly. If the pattern is not woven into the fabric, check that the design is printed correctly on the grain of the fabric. This is essential when the fabric is to be used for curtains, as the bottom hem must be turned up to the grain for the curtains to hang well.

(8) A large pattern repeat can be expensive, as extra material must be allowed for matching the pattern, and there may therefore be some wastage. It is more economical to choose a small pattern repeat, or a random design.

(9) Check fabrics carefully for flaws. These should be marked on the selvedge with a coloured thread. It is important to check for flaws before cutting into the fabric as some shops will not make allowances if the material has already been cut.

(10) Look at fabrics in daylight as well as in artificial light. If possible, take a large sample home and look at it in the setting for which it is intended.

(11) Consider some of the more unusual fabrics — felt, denim and mattress ticking. These are often a good choice when economy is necessary, or when furnishing children's bedrooms and playrooms.

(12) Make sure enough fabric is purchased for the work to be completed at the time. It is not always possible to obtain exact colour matches at a later date.

(13) Co-ordinated wallpapers and fabrics can be most effective. Spend a little time experimenting with these before making a final selection.

(14) Check the finish of the fabric, making sure that it has real body, not just a dressing that will come out the first time the fabric is washed or dry cleaned.

3

TOOLS AND EQUIPMENT

The Workbox

When buying new tools, always buy the best quality you can afford and use them only for the purpose for which they were intended. If scissors need sharpening have them professionally ground, or return them to the manufacturer for sharpening.

Keep tools and equipment in good working order. Replenish the workbox regularly with new pins and needles and look after them carefully. Bent needles result in poor workmanship, and rusty pins will mark fabrics.

Needles

Make sure the needle is sharp and free from rust. A selection of needles of various types for different fabrics should be kept in the workbox.

Sharps: These are used for general domestic sewing.

Betweens: These are similar to sharps but shorter. They are useful for quilting and when fine work has to be carried out in heavy fabrics.

Crewel or embroidery: They are the same length as sharps, but the long eye makes it easier to thread embroidery cotton and silk.

Mattress needles: These are curved, and therefore useful for upholstery and repairs.

Darners: Long needles with long eyes — easy to thread with wools or cottons.

Bodkins: Blunt, thick needles for threading elastic, cords etc. through casings.

Pins

Choose steel dressmaking pins. These will not pin-mark fabric. Glass headed pins are made from broken needles and are very sharp, so extra care is needed when using them. Do not leave pins in fabric longer that necessary, for they will mark the material. If a finger is pricked and blood accidentally stains the fabric, remove the stain by chewing a piece of tacking thread and rubbing it onto the bloodstain. This will remove the stain without leaving a water mark.

Threads

Try to match the thread to the fabric, but have it one tone darker. Use synthetic threads with synthetic fabrics. These are strong and can damage natural fibres. Cotton thread used on synthetic fibre would shrink more than synthetic fabric and cause it to pucker. For general use and for mediumweight fabrics of linen, cotton, etc. choose Sylko 40 or 50. Use stronger thread for heavier materials, silk or No.60 cotton for finer fabrics and tacking cotton for basting.

Scissors

These should be a large pair of dressmaking shears (20.5—23 cm, 8—9 in long) for cutting out, and a smaller pair (12.5—14 cm, 5—5½ in long) for cutting threads, etc. Choose the best quality possible.

Meter Stick

A wooden meter stick is required for measuring curtains accurately. A large set square is also useful for soft furnishing work.

Tape Measure

Choose a fibreglass or linen tape with a stiffened end. These are the most reliable as they will not stretch easily.

Tailor's Chalk

This is extremely useful when cutting out cushions, curtains and loose covers, and for marking pleats and darts. It is obtainable in several colours as well as white (though this is the easiest to remove).

'Quick Unpick'

This is a small ripping tool used for unpicking seams and stitches quickly.

Ironing Board and Iron

A wide board is the most useful, and a steam or heavy iron the most suitable, for home furnishings. Man-made fibres tend to leave marks on the base of the iron, so make sure the base is cleaned regularly.

Zipper Foot

This is a most useful attachment to any sewing machine, and invaluable when working with piping cord. It enables the stitching to be placed close to the piping and ensures a neat and accurate result. It is also used when inserting zip fasteners.

Thimble

Choose a metal one to protect the middle finger. Thimbles are particularly important when sewing firm fabric lampshades and coarse materials.

Sewing Machine

A sewing machine is essential for the making of soft furnishings, as many long seams often have to be worked. An electrically operated machine is an ideal choice as both hands can then be used to control the work.

A sewing machine should last a lifetime, so time and careful thought should be given to its selection. If possible choose a lightweight, versatile sewing machine with a free arm, and one capable of producing zigzag as well as straight stitching. Having bought it, make sure that you know how your machine operates. Practise using the attachments, and learn to be in complete control of it. Take advantage of any after-sales tuition that may be offered. Learn to thread up the machine quickly and accurately and to change the needles and feet to suit the fabric and thread being used. It pays to study the instruction booklets carefully.

Look after the machine. Clean and oil it regularly, and have it professionally serviced from time to time. Keep the machine covered when not in use and do not keep it in a cold, damp room or in direct heat. Never leave it with the electric plug connected, as this could burn out the motor.

4
STITCHES AND TECHNIQUES

Here are some of the stitches and techniques frequently used when making soft furnishings and other accessories for the home.

Stitches

Tacking (basting)

Tacking, or basting, is temporary stitching used to hold two or more thicknesses of fabric together. Stitch from right to left. There are two types of basting: *(1)* long equal stitches of about 1.3 cm (½ in) with equal space between *(fig. 2)* and *(2)* two stitches of 1.3 cm (½ in) and one stitch 2.5 cm (1 in) long *(fig. 3)*. The latter is particularly useful when tacking curtains. Start and finish both types of basting with a small back stitch.

Back stitch

This makes a strong seam. Stitch from right to left, taking the needle back the length of the stitch behind and bringing it through the length of the stitch in front. Keep the stitching even and approximately 6 mm (¼ in) in length *(fig. 4)*. This is a useful stitch, to be employed where the machine cannot work easily.

Prick stitch is very similar, but worked on the right side of the fabric. Only a very small back stitch is worked, and it is often used for inserting zips because it gives an unobtrusive line of stitching *(fig. 5)*.

Running stitch

This is worked on the right or wrong side of the fabric from right to left and is used when

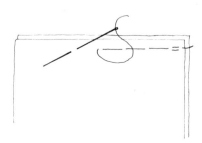

Fig. 2 *Tacking or basting, using long equal stitches*

Fig. 3 *Tacking using one long and two short stitches*

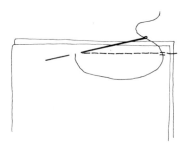

Fig. 4 *Back stitch*

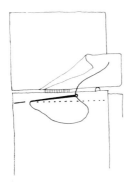

Fig. 5 *Prick stitch — used for inserting a zip fastener*

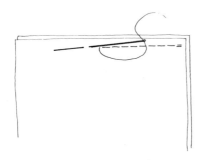

Fig. 6 *Running stitch*

Slip stitch
This is for joining folded edges together invisibly, as on a mitred corner. Pick up a thread from one fold and slide the needle through the fold for 6 mm (¼ in), and then put the needle into the other fold and carefully draw up the thread. Do not pull tightly (*fig. 9*).

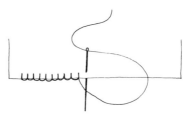

Fig. 7 *Blanket stitch*

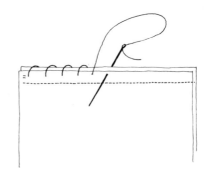

Fig. 8 *Neatening an edge with overcasting*

gathering by hand. Keep the stitches even, with equal spaces in between (*fig. 6*).

Bianket stitch
This is worked on the right side of the fabric, from left to right. It is often used to neaten a raw edge. It can also be used as a decorative stitch. Insert the needle at right angles through the fabric and bring it out to the edge of the fabric. Make a loop by keeping the thread under the needle (*fig. 7*).

Overcasting
This is used to neaten a raw edge to prevent fraying. Work from left to right, bringing the needle through at an acute angle and taking the thread over the raw edge (*fig. 8*).

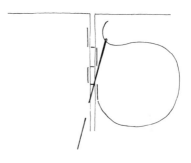

Fig. 9 *Slip stitch*

21

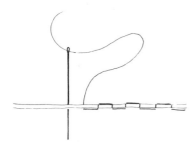

Fig. 10 *Stab stitch*

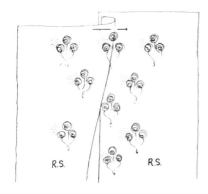

Fig. 11 *Pinning and matching the pattern before sliptacking*

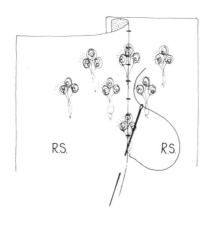

Fig. 12 *Sliptacking on the right side of the fabric*

Stab stitch
This is for joining two layers of fabric which are too thick for a normal seam. Insert the needle at right angles, making stitches approximately 6 mm (¼ in) long with an equal space in between (*fig. 10*).

Sliptacking (outside tacking)
This is used when patterns have to be matched accurately, and is worked on the right side of the fabric. It is particularly useful when matching patterns on curtains, loose covers and bedspreads. Fold in the edge of one piece of fabric on to its wrong side and place onto the right side of the piece of fabric to be matched. Pin into position, carefully matching the pattern. Sliptack, taking a stitch on the fold of the one side and slipping the needle down through the fold on the other (*figs. 11 and 12*).

Hemming
This is worked on the wrong side of the fabric and from right to left. Insert the needle just under the fold taking a thread of fabric, and then insert the needle into the hem. Do not pull the thread tightly (*fig. 13*).

Herringbone stitch
This is used for making hems on heavier fabrics where extra strength is necessary, and for securing interlining to the curtain fabric when making interlined curtains. The stitch is worked from left to right, usually over a raw edge. As it is also a decorative stitch it can be used successfully for appliqué. Keep the needle pointing to the left, and the thread on the right hand side of the stitching. Pick up first a thread of the folded fabric and then a thread of the single layer of fabric, keeping the stitches as near as possible to the raw edge (*fig. 14*).

Serging
This is used when turning down a single-fold hem round the raw edges of a curtain before the lining is applied. Sew from left to right,

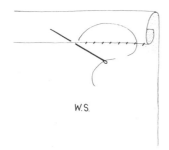

W.S.

Fig. 13 *Hemming*

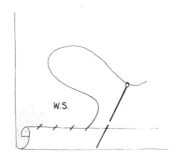

W.S.

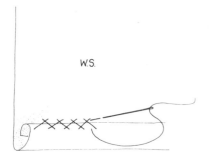

W.S.

Fig. 14 *Herringbone stitch*

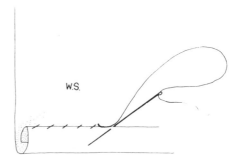

W.S.

Figs. 15 and 16 *Serging*

picking up a thread from the single thickness of fabric and then inserting the needle into the folded edge. The two stitches should be made in one movement and should be approximately 1.3 cm (½ in) in length. The stitches should not show on the right side of the fabric (*figs. 15 and 16*).

Lock stitch
This is a long, loose stitch approximately 10–15 cm (4–6 in) in length used to lock or secure the lining to a curtain. Work from left to right, using a long thread (*fig. 17*).

Seams

Plain flat seam
This is the most usual seam used in soft furnishings, and can be worked by machine or by using a backstitch. Place the fabric with raw

edges together, right sides facing, and tack 1.3 cm (½ in) from the edge. Stitch the seam, remove the tacking stitches and press open. Neaten the edges with a row of zigzag stitching along the raw edge, or overcast by hand (*fig. 18*). Alternatively, the seam can be neatened with seam binding.

When machining a curtain seam or other long seam always stitch down the length of the seam from the top to the bottom. Make sure that the nap (pile) runs in the same direction on each side of the seam — a point to watch particularly when sewing velvet. When machining on fine fabrics, p.v.c. or leather, use strips of tissue paper between the fabric and the machine presser foot to make stitching easier. Do not tack, or use pins, on p.v.c. or leather, as this will spoil the fabric. Instead, use sticky tape to hold the fabrics together whilst stitching.

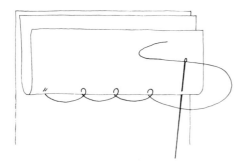

Fig. 17 *Lock stitch*

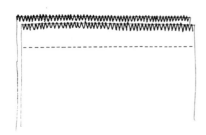

Fig. 18 *Plain flat seam. Edges neatened with a zigzag stitch*

French seam

This stitch is often used when widths of lightweight fabric are being joined together. It is suitable only for fabrics that are not thick and bulky. It is very strong and hard-wearing and is useful when making pillow cases, duvet covers, toilet bags and aprons. Place the two pieces of fabric together, wrong sides facing. Tack and stitch approximately 6 mm (¼ in) to 1.3 cm (½ in) in from the edge, depending on whether the fabric frays easily or not. Trim the seam and turn to the wrong side. With right sides together tack and machine to enclose the raw edges (*fig. 19*).

Flat fell seam

This is a useful seam when joining widths of fabric for unlined curtains or bedspreads, or where a strong enclosed seam is required. It is hard-wearing, but the stitching shows on the right side of the fabric. Place the wrong sides of the fabric together and have the raw edges even. Tack and machine 1.3 cm (½ in) in from the edge. Press seam open. Trim one side of the seam to 6 mm (¼ in) and turn in the raw edge of the other side 3 mm ($\frac{1}{8}$ in). Fold this over the trimmed edge and machine close to the fold (*figs. 20 and 21*).

Techniques

Mitred corners
A mitre is a fold used on hems when making curtains, pelmets, bedspreads, tablecloths, etc. It makes a smooth well-shaped corner and does not look bulky.

Folded mitres are used on the hems of lined and interlined curtains and on tablecloths. They can be perfect only when the two hems are the same width.

(a) Fold in the two hems the same width and press (*fig. 22*)

(b) Open out the hems so that they are flat and the fold marks are visible (*fig. 23*).

(c) Fold over the right side of the corner onto the wrong side of the fabric to make the first part of the mitre and press (*fig. 24*).

(d) Fold the hem again at the side and bottom to complete the mitre (*figs. 25 and 26*).

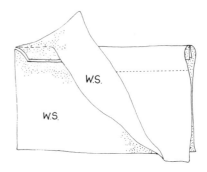

Fig. 19 *French seam showing raw edges enclosed*

24

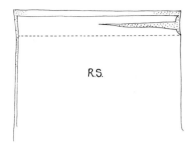

Fig. 20 *Trimming the seam allowance when making a flat fell seam*

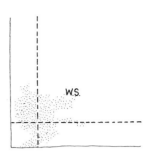

Fig. 23 *Hems opened out to show fold marks*

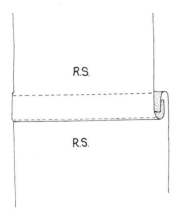

Fig. 21 *Completed flat fell seam*

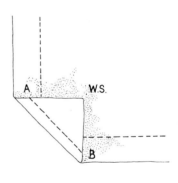

Fig. 24 *Folding the corner to make the first part of the mitre*

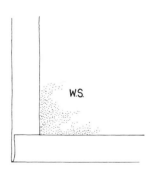

Fig. 22 *Folding and pressing hems of equal size to make a perfect mitre*

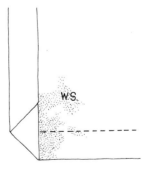

Fig. 25 *Folding in the side hem*

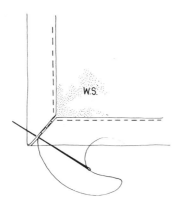

Fig. 26 *Lower hem folded to complete the mitre. Slipstitching the folds together*

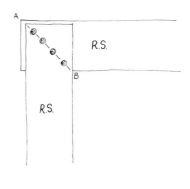

Fig. 28 *Tailor tacks made on Line A – B*

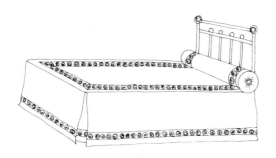

Fig. 27 *Contrast mitre used when making decorative borders*

If a thick fabric is being used, cut away some of the mitre to achieve a smoother finish. Cut away the fabric from A to B as in fig. 24.

Contrast mitres are used when making valances for beds and when making and applying decorative borders to curtains, loose covers and cushions. These borders can be made in contrasting fabrics and colours. This is a useful way of decorating plain or textured fabrics (*fig. 27*).

Decorative borders
Making and applying a border

(a) Cut strips of fabric equal in width and overlap them at right angles, making a line of tailor tacks from A to B (*fig. 28*). Cut tacks.

(b) Place right sides together and pin and tack along this line leaving the seam open 1.3 cm (½ in) at each end to enable the edges of the border to be folded in (*fig. 29*). Trim the seam to 1.3 cm (½ in) and press open.

(c) Turn under and press 1.3 cm (½ in) along the two raw edges of the border and apply to curtain, valance, etc. (*fig. 30*).

Braids, broderie anglaise and lace

Decorative braid on curtains, cushions, bedspreads, etc. is usually applied parallel to a straight edge. It is often necessary to mitre the corners, and if the pattern is very marked it should be matched if possible.

(a) Take two lengths of the braid, or lace, of equal width and overlap them at right angles (*fig. 31*). Fold under both ends of the braid, taking care to form the mitre at an angle of 45° (*fig. 31*). Press. Sliptack the two folds together on the right side (*fig. 32*).

(b) Stitch along the tacking line on the wrong side. Trim seams and press flat. Neaten the raw edges by oversewing.

Decorative cord

Furnishing cord is made up of three or four thick cotton or silk strands twisted together, and is similar in appearance to piping cord. It

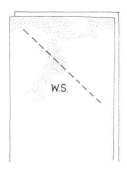

Fig. 29   *Machine line leaving ends of seam open 1.3 cm (½ in)*

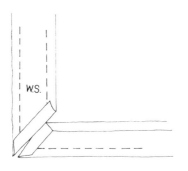

Fig. 30   *Turning in 1.3 cm (½ in) along raw edge, showing lines of folds*

has the advantage of being less expensive than most decorative braids and can be used most effectively on curtains, cushions and many other items in the home. As it is often applied to the edge of a cushion or a curtain it cannot be tacked on first, so extra care is needed when sewing it.

(a) Bind the end of the cord with thread to prevent its unravelling. If it is being used on a cushion, a small gap can be left in the seam and the ends inserted into it.

(b) With the right side of the fabric facing, place the cord onto the edge of the fabric holding it with the left hand.

(c) Pick up 3 mm ($\frac{1}{8}$ in) on the fold of the fabric and insert the needle behind three strands of the cord. Take the needle back again into the fold and continue stitching (*fig. 33*).

Ricrac braids

These have many decorative uses in the home and can be used on table linen and other household items. The braid should be tacked into position on the right side of the fabric first, and then machined into position. Alternatively, it can be stitched on by hand using embroidery thread and couching stitch (*fig. 35*); this makes a very decorative edge.

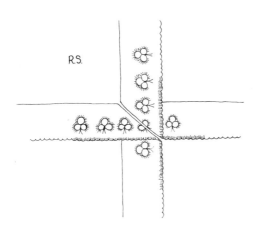

Fig. 31   *Mitring the corners and matching the pattern of broderie anglaise*

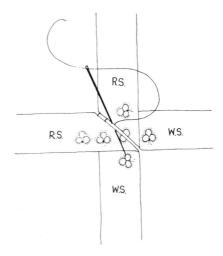

Fig. 32   *Decorative braid folded to form mitre*

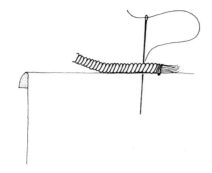

Fig. 33   *Applying a decorative cord*

Fig. 34   *Tacking on ricrac braid*

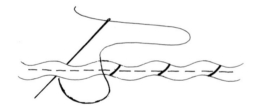

Fig. 35   *Couch stitch used when sewing on ricrac braid*

Find the length into which an even number of scallops can be marked by folding and cutting out the paper as in fig. 36. Alternatively, draw out the design required, using a large plate or saucer so that it fits into the length of the paper pattern.

(b)   Pin the pattern to the fabric and mark out with tailor's chalk on its right side. Cut out, making turning allowances where necessary (*fig. 37*).

To face or line a scalloped edge, cut a piece of lining fabric the same size as the top fabric. Place right sides of fabric and lining together and tack round the scalloped edge. Machine stitch into position, trim the seams and clip the curves (*fig. 38*). Turn to right side, and press. If required, the edges of the scallops can then be topstitched 6 mm (¼ in) from the edges.

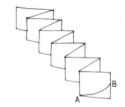

Fig. 36   *Paper pattern folded to find the length of scallops showing cutting line A – B*

Edges

Scalloped edges
Scalloped edges can be used as a decorative finish for roller blinds, table linen, bedspreads, lampshades and other household accessories. The edges can be bound with bias binding or crossway strip, faced, or finished with decorative machine stitching or trimming. To make the scallops:

(a)   Make a pattern from a piece of paper the length of the edge to be scalloped.

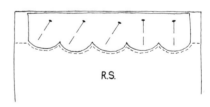

Fig. 37   *Paper pattern pinned to the right side of the fabric and marked for scallops*

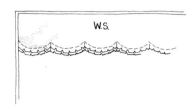

Fig. 38 *Lining machined into position*

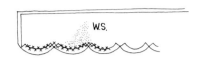

Fig. 39 *Fabric herringbone stitched to interfacing on the wrong side*

When a firm finish is required (e.g. scalloped edge for a fitted bedspread) the edge can be interlined with a lightweight non-woven interfacing (Vilene). This should be cut to the exact size of the paper pattern, omitting any turning allowance, and lined as above.

If an even stiffer result is required (e.g. dressing table pelmet) use a heavyweight interfacing. Cut this to the required size and turn the right side of the fabric onto the interfacing and herringbone round the scalloped edge (*fig. 39*).

When finishing a single layer of fabric with a scalloped edge and decorative stitching (e.g. tablecloth, napkins) first draw out the scallop deisgn on the fabric. For a really professional finish make two runs of machine stitching along this edge. *1st run*: Machine along the scallop using large, close zigzag stitch (satin stitch), and having thin paper underneath. Remove the paper and cut round the scallops carefully. *2nd run*: Machine the edge with a small zigzag stitch. If possible, guide a piece of pearl cord along the edge when stitching, taking care that it does not slip over or under it. Use paper underneath (*fig. 40*).

Automatic machine scalloping. This is an easy way to form small scallops using an automatic machine with built-in embroidery stitch. Set the machine to the scalloping stitch and to satin stitch, and work round the edge of the fabric. When complete, cut away surplus fabric close to the stitching. Using an automatic embroidery stitch makes

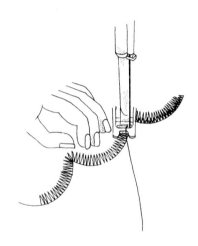

Fig. 40 *Second row of machine stitching showing cord applied to the edge using a small zigzag stitch*

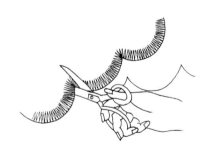

Fig. 41 *Cutting away the fabric close to the stitching*

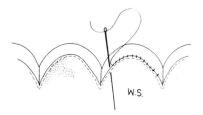

Fig. 42 *Hemming bias strip into position, showing fullness mitred between each scallop*

Fig. 44 *Pinning pleats into position*

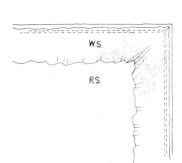

Fig. 43 *Applying the frill to the right side of the fabric, allowing extra fullness at the corners*

small scallops. This type of edge would be best used on smaller household items such as table linen and lampshades (*fig. 41*).

Binding the scallops. To bind the edge of a scallop prepare crossway strips or bias binding the required length. Place the edges of the binding to the right side of the fabric and tack and machine on the seam line. Trim seam and snip curves. Turn the binding to the wrong side of the fabric, then turn in the raw edge and hem into position, mitring the fullness between each scallop, and press (*fig. 42*).

Frills

A gathered or pleated frill can be used to decorate such items as cushions, pillowcases, bedspreads and cots. The frill varies in size depending on the item being trimmed. Narrow frills are usually made from double fabric.

Gathered frill. To make a 7.5 cm (3 in) frill cut a piece of fabric 1½ to 2 times the length of the edge to be frilled, if necessary joining the fabric pieces. If making a continuous frill for a cushion or a pillowcase, join the short edges of the strip together, fold and press in half lengthwise and make two rows of gathering stitches 6 mm (¼ in) from the raw edges. If a long frill is being made divide the strip into sections. This prevents the threads breaking and enables the gathers to be evenly distributed. With right sides together, pin and tack the frill to the fabric being trimmed and arrange the gathers evenly, but allow slightly more fullness at any corners (*fig. 43*). Tack and machine into position.

Pleated frills. Cut out and prepare the strips of fabric as for the gathered frill, but allow three times the length if making knife or box pleats without a space between. Pin into pleats, measuring accurately (*fig. 44*). Tack and press. Make two rows of machine stitching 6 mm (¼ in) from the raw edges to hold the pleats into position. Apply to the fabric as for the gathered frill.

Piping and Cutting on the Cross

Strips of fabric cut on the bias or cross grain of the material are essential when making soft furnishings and accessories for the home. As well as being used to cover piping cord and strengthen seams, crossway strip is often used for binding raw seams and making decorative edges. Fabric cut on the cross has more give, and is much more flexible than that cut on the straight of the grain. It is therefore much easier to apply it to a curved edge. However, once stretched it will not spring back to its original size, so care must be taken when using it. To be really successful it must always be cut on the true bias or cross of the fabric.

Piped edge

Piping cord covered with crossway (bias) strips can be sewn into the seams of cushions, loose covers and bedspreads. This strengthens the seams and at the same time defines the shape of the article and gives a decorative finish.

Piping cord is usually made from cotton, and is available in various thicknesses. The thickness of the cord used must depend on the article being made and the weight and texture of the fabric.

No. 1 (fine): Used when cushion covers and accessories are made from very fine, lightweight fabrics. Use strips of crossway 2.5 cm (1 in) wide to cover this narrow cord.

Nos. 2, 3 and 4 (medium): Normally used when making loose covers, bedspreads and cushion covers. Use strips of crossway 3.8 cm (1½ in) wide to cover them.

Nos. 5, 6 (coarse): Used where a thick decorative edging is required. A wider strip of fabric is required when working with these.

Piping cord should be carefully shrunk before use, otherwise when washed it will shrink, and the strips of fabric covering it will pucker. Most piping cord is sold as shrink resistant, but, if no guarantee is given, shrink it yourself by boiling it for five minutes in a saucepan of water, drying it thoroughly before use.

The crossway strips used for covering piping cord can be made in matching or contrasting colours, but the texture and weight of the fabric should be similar to the article being made. Loosely woven fabric is not suitable, as it wears too quickly.

Cutting fabric on the cross

(a) Fold the material diagonally so that the selvedge thread lies across the cross-

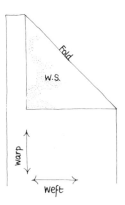

Fig. 45 *Folding the fabric to find the true cross grain*

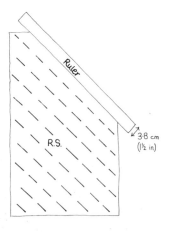

Fig. 46 *Marking parallel lines on the fabric using a rigid rule*

ways thread, i.e. the warp across the weft (*fig. 45*). Press. Cut along the fold. The material is the on the true bias or cross grain.

(b) In order to make all the strips exactly the same size, make a ruler in stiff card 3.8 cm (1½ in) wide to use as a guide. This is the most usual size of strip used in soft furnishings and accessories for the home. A narrower ruler, 2.5 cm (1 in) wide, can be used when cutting strips to bind seams and make decorative edgings.

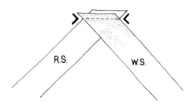

Fig. 47 *Joining crossway strips on the straight grain. Note the angle*

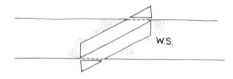

Fig. 48 *The join showing the seam pressed open and the corners trimmed*

(c) Place the edge of the ruler to the cut edge of the fabric and mark with a sharp piece of tailor's chalk, making parallel lines the same width. Cut along the lines. Continue until sufficient strips have been made (*fig. 46*).

Joining the crossway strips
All joins made on crossway strips should be made on the straight grain of the fabric. Place two strips together with right sides facing and pin and stitch the seam, making sure that the strips form an angle as shown in fig. 47. Press the seam open and trim away the corners (*fig. 48*).

Quick method of cutting on the cross
When several metres of crossway strips are required it is useful to be able to prepare it without having to join each strip separately. This simple method can save many hours of work.

(a) Take a strip of fabric 23 cm (9 in) wide. The length of the strip should be at least twice the width (i.e. 46 cm, 18 in) or more.

(b) Fold over the top right-hand corner to obtain the direct cross (*fig. 49*). Cut off this corner and join the lower edge with 6 mm (¼ in) seam (*fig. 50*). By adding this piece no fabric is wasted.

(c) With a ruler 3.8 cm (1½ in) wide, mark lines on the right side of the fabric with a sharp piece of tailor's chalk, parallel to the top edge. Mark also a 6 mm (¼ in) seam allowance down each side and mark the first and second lines A and B as in fig. 51.

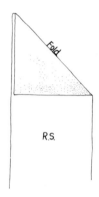

Fig. 49 *Folding the fabric to obtain the direct cross*

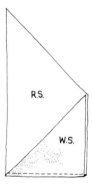

Fig. 50 *Cut-off corner joined to the lower edge*

(d) Take a pin through the wrong side of the fabric at point A and take this across to point B, pinning very accurately with right sides together. Continue pinning along the seam. Tack and stitch the seam, checking first that the lines match up exactly. This makes a tube. Press seam open.

(e) Turn to the right side and start cutting round the tube at the projecting strip at the top edge (*fig. 52*).

A length of 23 cm (9 in) of fabric 91.5 cm (36 in) wide makes approximately 5 metres (5½ yd) of crossway strip 3.8 cm (1½ in) wide.

If larger pieces of fabric are available the top right-hand corner and the bottom left-hand corner can be cut off and set aside. This produces the same shaped piece of fabric but has the advantage of having fewer joins in the tube. Remember that the length of the strip of fabric must be at least twice the width (*fig. 53*).

Square pieces of fabric can be utilised in a similar way by cutting and joining as in figs. 54 and 55, placing AB to CD with right sides together.

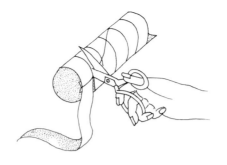

Fig. 52 *Cutting round the tube starting at the projecting strip at the top edge*

Fig. 53 *Alternative method of cutting using a wider, longer piece of fabric*

Fig. 51 *Lines marked parallel to the top edge. Seam pressed open*

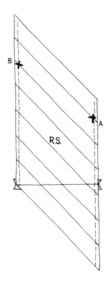

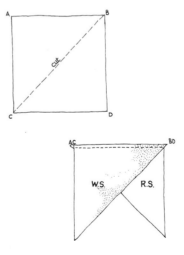

Figs. 54 and 55 *Using a square piece of fabric*

33

Application of piping

(a) When crossway strip is used to cover piping cord, cut the beginning of the strip diagonally on the straight grain of the fabric. Run the thumb gently down the length of the strip to take out a little of the stretch. Fold the strip in half lengthways with wrong sides together and insert the piping cord, leaving the end of the cord extending beyond the strip.

(b) Start to apply the piping along a straight edge — never on a corner. Tack with matching thread, keeping the stitches close to the cord and all the raw edges even. These stitches can remain in the finished work (*fig. 56*).

(c) To turn a corner neatly only one slash is usually required. Make a clip 1.3 cm (½ in) in from the corner and work a small backstitch to strengthen it (*fig. 57*).

(d) To pipe round a curved edge clip the crossway strip before applying the piping. This ensures that the strip moulds and sets well to the shape required. Work a backstitch at each clip for extra strength (*fig. 58*).

To make a join

(a) To join the two ends of the piping so that they fit neatly, open the stitching at the beginning of the piping for 5 cm (2 in). Check that the crossway is cut diagonally across so that the edge is on the straight grain of the fabric. Mark a line 2.5 cm (1 in) in from this raw edge using tailor's chalk, keeping the line parallel (*fig. 59*).

(b) Place the other end of the crossway strip onto the chalk line, fold back onto this line at a right angle, and cut off (*fig. 60*). This allows 1.3 cm (½ in) turnings for the seam.

(c) Join the two ends of the strip with right sides together, making a 1.3 cm (½ in) seam. It is important to make this seam exactly 1.3 cm (½ in) in width or the

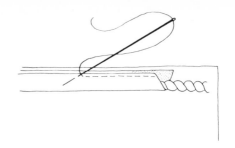

Fig. 56 *Applying crossway strip and piping cord, keeping raw edges level*

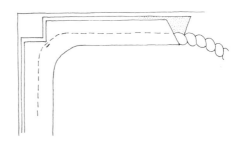

Fig. 57 *Making a slash to turn a corner neatly*

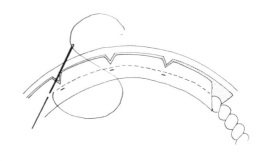

Fig. 58 *Applying piping to a curved edge*

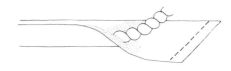

Fig. 59 *Making a line 2.5 cm (1 in) from the diagonally cut raw edge*

1 *Co-ordinating fabrics used for tablecloths and roller blind*

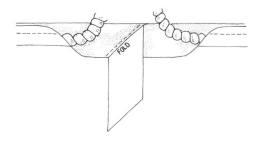

Fig. 60 *Crossway strip folded diagonally to form a right angle*

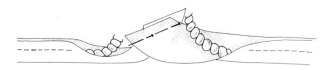

Fig. 61 *Joining crossway strips with 1.3 cm (½ in) turnings*

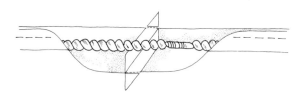

Fig. 62 *Seam pressed open showing join in piping cord*

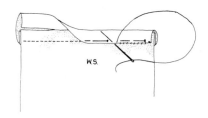

Fig. 63 *Hemstitching the bound edge to the wrong side on the machine line*

piping will not fit properly. Stitch the seam and trim down to 6 mm (¼ in) on smaller items. Press seam open, and trim corners *(fig. 62)*.

(d) To join the piping cord cut the two ends so that they butt together and do not overlap. Bind with thread to hold them together, or join as follows: *(i)* Unravel the cord for 2.5 cm (1 in) on each side. Cut away one strand from one side and two strands from the other side. *(ii)* Wind the remaining three strands together and stitch neatly.

Bound Edge

A bound edge is made from strips of fabric cut on the bias or cross grain of the fabric and should be cut three times the required finished width. Usually a strip 3.8—5 cm (1½—2 in) is wide enough.

(a) Prepare strips of fabric using the method described in the earlier section on cutting fabric on the cross or, if large quantities are needed, use the quick method of cutting. Remember to join the strips together on the straight of the grain. *(figs. 47 and 48)*.

(b) Place the edge of the crossway strip to the right side of the edge to be bound. Tack and machine 1.3 cm (½ in) from the raw edges *(fig. 63)*.

(c) Turn the strip to the wrong side and fold in 1.3 cm (½ in). Pin and tack so that the fold comes onto the line of machine stitching. Hem by hand so that the stitches are worked on the machine line *(fig. 63)*.

5

CURTAINS AND ROLLER BLINDS

Curtains and blinds can do much to furnish a room, as they often provide the greatest amount of colour, texture and style and set the scene for other furnishings and accessories.

Many different effects can be achieved by the use of various tracks, poles and fittings, and by treating the window with pelmets, blinds or full length curtains. Illusions of height and width can be achieved if careful thought is given to the planning of windows and doors.

Bay windows and bow windows often need to be treated quite separately from other windows and doors in a room. If, however, more than two curtains are used, try using a valance or pelmet to knit the unit together.

When treating a dormer window consider using a roller blind and a small pair of dress curtains to match. These are fixed at the side of the windows and used purely for decoration. They cannot be drawn as they do not have enough width for actual use. If matching wallpaper is used for the surrounding alcove an attractive effect can be achieved.

Roller blinds are economical to make and can be a very practical way of treating kitchen and bathroom windows, as they can be sponged clean. They look effective when used with pelmets or small dress curtains.

Floor length curtains look best in most rooms, but of course take more fabric. Short curtains can be used effectively in cottagy-style rooms and small rooms, but try to use long curtains in living rooms, dining rooms and main bedrooms.

Keep curtains as clean as possible by brushing and vacuuming them regularly. One pair of curtains may have three different fabrics — face fabric, interlining and lining fabric — and each may need different cleaning techniques.

Care should be taken to select fabrics for curtains that suit both the decorative scheme and the purpose for which they are needed. (See Chapter 2.)

Curtain Tracks and Fittings

There are many different tracks, rods, poles and fittings to choose from and these have been improved and developed over the last few years. Several manufacturers produce helpful booklets on the many fittings and accessories available, and these should be studied carefully before a choice is made. Some tracks and rods are easier to fix to the wall than others, and some have combined hooks and runners. Other tracks have cording systems. Not all tracks are equally pleasing to the eye, but some can be covered successfully with curtain fabric or wallpaper, or a pelmet or valance made to cover them.

Some plastic tracks are not strong enough to take the weight of heavy interlined curtains, so check on the strength of the tracks and fittings.

Linings

Most curtains are enhanced by a lining. As well as enabling the curtain to drape well, it

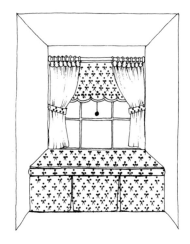

(i)

(iii)

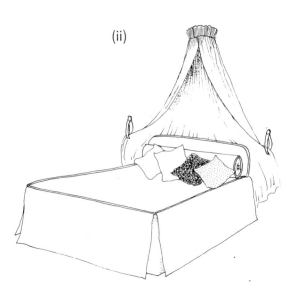

(ii)

Fig. 64 *Ideas for curtains*
   *(i)   Treating a dormer window. Matching
         curtains roller blind and window seat*
   (ii) Making a bed canopy
   *(iii) Matching curtains round bath and
         vanitory unit. These are fixed onto
         a flexible track*
   *(iv) Contrast border used on side and
         lower edges of curtain. Coloured
         curtain linings can be used effectively*
   (v)   Use of a pole for a double glazed door

helps to protect the curtain fabric from sunlight, dust and frost. All these damage the fibres of the fabric and make it wear out more quickly.

Choose a good quality cotton sateen for lining. A poor quality lining is a false economy as it will wear out before the curtain. Many colours are available, including natural and white. Also available is metal insulated fabric which is completely draughtproof, making it a particularly good choice when preparing curtains for doors.

Detachable linings can be made for curtains, using a special curtain lining tape. These linings are easily removed for washing and can be changed from one pair of curtains to another. The lining is made separately from the curtains and has its own tape. It is attached to the curtain by the same hooks which suspend the curtain from the track. These linings

(iv)

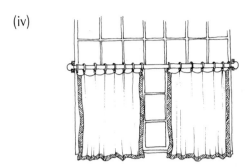

(v)

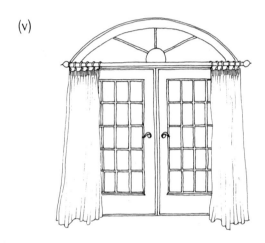

do not have the same professional finish as permanently lined curtains and they do not hang or drape as well, but they are useful in cases when curtains need to be washed frequently.

Interlinings

Interlined curtains have all the advantages of lined curtains and more. As well as helping the curtains to drape well, the interlining causes the texture or pattern of the fabric to be shown to the best advantage. It is particularly advantageous when thinner fabrics such as silk or dupion have been used, as the interlining gives the fabric body. It is a very good insulator, keeping out both cold and noise. Use bump or domette for interlining. (See Chapter 2.)

Measuring and Estimating

When the curtain tracks or decorative rods have been chosen and fixed into position, it is possible to estimate the amount of fabric required. The track or rod is usually placed 5—10 cm (2—4 in) above the window frame and should be extended 15—45.5 cm (6—18 in) at each side of the frame, depending on the width of the window and the thickness of the curtain fabric. A wide window will need more room at each side to accommodate the curtains when drawn back. Heavily interlined curtains also take up more space at either side of a window.

Measure the window carefully and decide on the exact position of the track or pole. A pole is a decorative feature and the curtains should hang below it. Use a wooden metre stick or rigid rule, as accurate measurements cannot be obtained with a tape measure. Draw a diagram and mark in all the appropriate measurements.

If the curtains are to hang to the sill they should end 5—10 cm (2—4 in) below the sill (or actually *on* the sill in a few cases). If they are to hang to the floor they should finish within 1.3 cm (½ in) of the floor covering. Avoid any in-between measurement as the curtains will look out of proportion to the window and this will spoil the finished effect.

Two measurements are necessary to estimate the amount of fabric needed:
(1) The width of the track (not the window) measured from end to end.
(2) The finished length of the curtains, i.e. the drop, measured from the position from which the curtains will hang to the required bottom edge. To these measurements must be added an allowance for turnings for hems and headings. Allow 15—23 cm (6—9 in) inclusive.

When using patterned fabric allow an extra pattern repeat on each 'drop' of curtain when cutting. All the curtains should finish at the same position of the pattern. Plan them so that the pattern starts at their lower edge after making an allowance for the hem.

Decide how many widths of fabric will be required to give the curtains the fullness you require. This will depend on the weight and thickness of the fabric chosen and the heading selected. Remember that light, unlined curtains should have more fullness than heavy interlined ones. Here is a useful guide:

(1) Simple gathered headings require approximately one and a half times the width of the track.
(2) Pinch pleats require from two to two-and-a-half times the width of the track.
(3) Pencil pleats and many of the other commercial headings require from two-and-a half to three times the width of the track.

To obtain the required fullness it is often necessary to join widths or half widths together. Any half widths that have to be used should be joined so that they will hang at the outer sides of the window.

Take care when matching and joining patterns. Pin and tack on the outside of the fabric to obtain an accurate match (*figs. 11 and 12*).

The same amount of fabric will be needed for the lining as for curtains.

Making the Curtains

It is important to observe a few important rules when cutting out fabric for curtains and blinds.

(1) Use a large square or rectangular table for cutting out so that the end of the table can be used to square up the fabric if necessary.
(2) If possible, draw a thread in order to get a straight line for cutting. It is not possible to draw threads on all fabrics; in this case square up the fabric with the table or use a large set square to obtain an accurate cutting line.
(3) Cut plain fabric to the grain of the material. Where a patterned fabric is incorrectly printed, cut to the pattern and not to the grain.

(4) Cut out each length of curtain taking care to match the patterns. Mark with pins or tailor's chalk. Allow for pattern repeats and turnings, and check these carefully before cutting.
(5) Cut off all selvedges, for these often make the seams pucker.
(6) Prepare the side and bottom hems of the curtains first. The curtains should then be measured to the required finished length and the heading applied last.

Unlined Curtains

(1) Cut out the fabric, matching the patterns carefully. Cut off selvedges. Join widths where necessary, using a flat fell seam (*figs. 20 and 21*).
(2) At the side edges of the curtains fold and tack 1.3 cm (½ in) double hems. Machine stitch to ensure a firm edge.
(3) Fold up 5 cm (2 in) at the bottom edge of the curtain to make a 2.5 cm (1 in) double hem (*fig. 65*). Tack and machine, taking care to make a neat finish on the right side of the curtain.
(4) Apply tape as required. (See the section later in this chapter.)

Lined Curtains

(1) Cut out the fabric matching patterns carefully and cutting off all selvedges. Join widths or half widths of fabric with a plain flat seam (*fig. 18*) and press open. Do not neaten the edges.
(2) Fold in 3.8 cm (1½ in) at the sides and lower edges of the curtain and tack. Mitre the two lower corners (*figs. 22–26*) and slipstitch. Using matching single thread, serge stitch (*figs. 15 and 16*) the two side hems and the lower hem.
(3) Cut the lining sateen to the same size as the curtain fabric, removing all selvedges. Join widths or half widths as necessary, using a plain flat seam. Press open.
(4) Press the curtain carefully and place it on a large table with the wrong side

uppermost. Press the lining and apply it to the curtain with wrong sides together, matching the seams of the lining to the seams of the curtain where possible.

(5) Lock the lining to the curtain fabric to ensure that it hangs well and does not fall away from the curtain fabric (*fig. 17*). Locking stitches are long loose stitches made so that they do not pull and therefore pucker the curtain. Two or three rows of locking stitches should be made in every width of 122 cm (48 in) wide fabric. Match the thread to the curtain fabric and not the lining. Fold back the lining at the centre of the curtain and lock into position, making stitches every 10–15 cm (4–6 in). (*fig. 66*).

(6) Trim off lining at side edges of the curtain so that it is flush with the curtain. Fold in the lining 2.5 cm (1 in) at the lower edge and at the two side edges making sure that the corner of the lining meets the mitre on the curtain. Tack round the two sides and lower edge.

(7) Work a row of tacking stitches across the curtain 15 cm (6 in) from the top edge. This keeps the lining in position while the heading is worked.

(8) Slipstitch the lining to the curtain at the two sides and lower edge (*fig. 9*) using matching thread, leaving the top 15 cm (6 in) of the curtain unstitched to allow for the heading to be worked.

(9) Apply tape as required. (See the section later in this chapter.)

Interlined Curtains

(1) Cut out the curtains and the lining as for lined curtains. Cut the interlining to the same size as the curtain fabric and join widths and half widths as necessary. As bump and domette tend to stretch, make the join with a lapped seam using two rows of zigzag machine stitching (*fig. 67*).

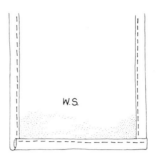

Fig. 65 *Making a 1.3 cm (½ in) double hem at side edges and a 2.5 cm (1 in) double hem at the lower edge of an unlined curtain*

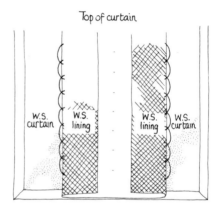

Fig. 66 *The lining lockstitched to the curtain fabric and worked from the top to the bottom of the curtain*

(2) Place the curtain fabric on a large table with the wrong side uppermost. Lay the interlining on the wrong side of the curtain matching sides and lower edges. Fold back the interlining at the centre of the curtain and lockstitch into position as for lined curtains (*fig. 66*), making two rows of locking stitches to every piece of 122 cm (48 in) width fabric.

41

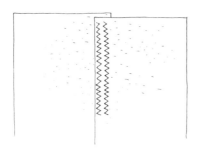

Fig. 67 *Joining interlining fabric with a lapped seam*

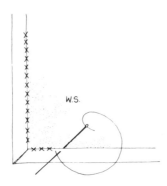

W.S.

Fig. 68 *Hems on an interlined curtain being stitched into position using herringbone stitch*

(3) Turn in 5 cm (2 in) at each side of the curtain and at the bottom edge, folding both the interlining and the curtain fabric together. Mitre the two corners, cutting away the bump if the corner is too bulky. Tack and herringbone stitch the hems into position to make a firm edge (*fig. 68*). Slipstitch the mitred corners.

(4) Place the lining on top of the interlining right side up and work two rows of locking stitches as for lined curtains. Fold in the lining 3.8 cm (1½ in) at the side and bottom edges of the curtain, matching mitres, and finish as for lined curtains.

(5) Apply tape as required. If the heading is too bulky to pleat, the interlining can be cut off to the required depth of the heading at the top of the curtain.

Curtain Headings

There are many decorative curtain heading tapes on the market and new ones are often introduced. They are a great help to the curtain maker as they are quick and easy to apply. The hooks from the tape can be removed easily when the curtains need to be washed or dry cleaned.

The pleating or gathering produced by commercial tapes is usually achieved by pulling up cords in the tape or by inserting special pleater hooks into the tape at regular intervals. Single, double and triple pleats can be made with such hooks. Generally speaking, the use of pleater hooks gives a crisper effect than that produced by tapes that are simply pulled up with cords.

1. Gathered heading

This standard pocketed tape 2.5 cm (1 in) wide produces a simple gathered heading suitable for use under pelmets or valances where the heading does not show. It can also be used on simple lined and unlined curtains when only a narrow frill is required above the heading. For a really crisp finish, a strip of stiffening such as iron-on bonded interfacing (Vilene) or buckram can be inserted into the fold at the top of the curtain before the tape is applied.

This tape can be obtained in both cotton and man-made fibres for use with lighter fabrics and nets and sheers. Allow at least one-and-a-half times the width of the track when estimating for the curtain fabric.

Applying the tape — without a frill

(a) Measure the width of the curtain to obtain the amount of tape required and allow 2.5 cm (1 in) turnings at each end.

(b) Size up the curtains by measuring from their bottom edge to obtain the correct position for the tape. Measure along the curtain every 30.5 cm (12 in) to obtain an accurate result. For a curtain without a frill the tape is sewn in position 6 mm (¼ in) from the top edge, and any extra fabric is turned in at the top.

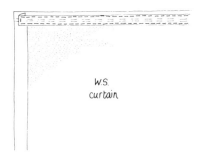

Fig. 69 *Heading tape machined into position*

Such curtains can then be lengthened, if necessary, by removing the tape and extending from the top edge, thus avoiding a mark at the bottom hem.

(c) Cut the heading tape to the width of the curtain plus 2.5 cm (1 in) for turnings at each end.

(d) Tack the heading tape into position at the top edge of the curtain, turning in 1.3 cm (½ in) of tape at each end to neaten. Pull out the cords at each end and knot together.

(e) Machine along top and bottom edges of tape and along the two ends (*fig. 69*). When machining tapes to curtains, always stitch along the top edge of the tape first. Take out of the machine and make the second line of stitching at the lower edge of the tape in the same direction. This prevents the heading from puckering.

(f) Insert hooks into the tape approximately every 7.5—10 cm (3½—4 in) and draw up the cords on the outside edge of the curtain distributing the gathers evenly. Do not cut off the cord but tie neatly into a large bow or use a cord tidy. These can be released easily for washing or dry cleaning of the curtains.

Applying the tape — to make a frill

(a) Measure the width of the curtain to obtain the amount of tape required and allow 2.5 cm (1 in) turnings at each end.

(b) Size up the curtains to obtain the correct position for the tape and allow 5—7.5 cm (2—3 in) extra length to make the frill.

(c) Tack the heading to the top edge of the curtain covering the raw edges. Fold over onto the lining to the depth of the frill required, usually about 2.5—5 cm (1—2 in). To make a stiffer heading, cut a piece of interfacing or Vilene and insert this into the fold at the top of the curtain. Pin, tack and machine stitch all round the tape and finish as in fig. 70.

2. Pencil pleats

Pencil pleats are produced by drawing up cords on specially stiffened tape, and require two-and-a-half to three times the width of the track. The tape is approximately 7.5 cm (3 in) deep and is made in cotton and man-made fibres to suit both heavy and light-weight curtain fabrics.

The tape is sewn to the curtain 6 mm (¼ in) from the top edge and should be applied as for a gathered heading without a frill. (See the earlier section in this chapter.) Make sure that the tape is applied with the pockets in their correct position, according to whether or not the track or pole is to show above the curtain heading.

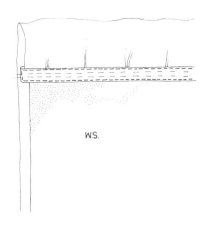

Fig. 70 *Making a frill at the top of the curtain*

3. Pinch pleats

Pinch pleats can be achieved by using either one of two different types of tape. One tape draws up sets of pleats along the curtain automatically, leaving a space between each set of pleats (*fig. 71*). The other tape has pockets all along it, the width of the curtain being reduced and pleated by insertion of special long-pronged pleater hooks into the pockets. When using this tape it is important to work out the approximate width down to which the fabric will pleat. The following example gives a rough guide, but it is best to pleat up the tape before applying it in order to work out the formula for the individual curtain. Arrange the hooks so that there is a single pleat at each end of the curtain. The rest of the hooks should be spaced out evenly across the curtain. Use four-pronged hooks for making triple pleats, three-pronged for making double pleats and two-pronged hooks for making single pleats (*fig. 72*).

example:
122 cm (48 in) fabric pleats down to:

single pleat	double pleat	triple pleat
66 cm	61 cm	58.5 cm
(26 in)	(24 in)	(23 in)

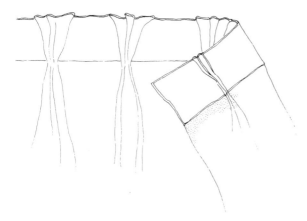

Fig. 71 *9 cm (3½ in) pinch pleats made by pulling up the cords on the curtain tape, for example, Rufflette Autopleat*

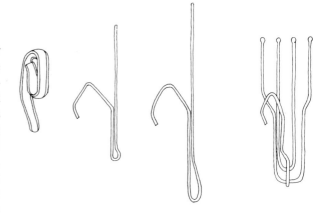

Fig. 72 *Curtain hooks for commercial tapes*

When estimating fabric requirements remember that these tapes use two-and-a-half times the width of the track according to the tape used and whether single, double or triple pleating is required. Most of the pinch pleat tapes are available in both cotton and synthetic fibres for use with either heavy or lightweight fabrics.

Sew the tape on to the curtain 6 mm (¼ in) from the top edge and follow the instructions for a gathered heading without a frill given earlier in this chapter. Make sure that the tape is applied with the pockets in their correct position.

Roller Blinds

Roller blinds are easy and inexpensive to make at home and they are more practical than curtains in kitchens and bathrooms. They roll right up to the top of the window to give the maximum light by day.

Roller blind kits are obtainable at do-it-yourself shops and many large stores. Special holland fabric should be used to make the blind, as this is quick and easy to use and does not fray at the edges. It repels dirt and dust and can be sponged clean. It is made in wide widths so that joining is often unnecessary.

Closely woven furnishing cottons and linens can also be used for making blinds but need to be strengthened first with a fabric stiffener. This can either be sprayed on to the fabric from an aerosol can, or the fabric can be dipped into a liquid stiffener. Test a small piece of the fabric first to check how much stiffening is required.

Make the blind from one width of fabric if possible. For a wide window the fabric can be used sideways if the pattern allows. If necessary, make two or even three blinds for a very wide window. Seams in blinds are not always satisfactory as they make the fabric too thick and stop the roller from working smoothly. With commercially stiffened fabrics that do not fray it is not necessary to have side hems as this also adds thickness to the blind. However, if a fabric stiffener is used it may be necessary to turn in the side hem 1.3 cm (½ in) and machine into position using a zig zag stitch (or two rows of straight stitch). When machining, keep the fabric as flat as possible as the stiffened fabric can crack if folded.

The lower edge of the blind may be finished in many ways. A shaped edge can be made and fixed to the bottom edge or a decorative braid or fringe can be used (*fig. 73*). Pull cords can be obtained in various styles or a handmade knotted or plaited cord could be applied (*fig. 74*).

Plain blinds can be decorated with fabric paints using freehand designs or stencils (*fig. 75*). These are most effective as they can be designed to co-ordinate with tiles, fabrics, etc. in the room. Stencils in many designs can be purchased for this purpose and are made from paper or plastic. A stencil brush should be used to apply the special fabric paint, which can be obtained from good art and craft shops. Secure the stencil firmly to the blind using double sided self-adhesive tape or masking tape before painting on the design. Practise stencilling first on a small piece of blind fabric before painting the design on the blind itself.

Fig. 73 *Some finishes for roller blinds*

Fig. 74 *Pull cords for roller blinds*

Fig. 75 *Roller blinds decorated with fabric paint to create original designs*

45

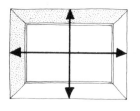 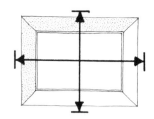

Fig. 76 *Positions for roller blinds*

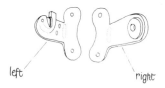

left   right

Fig. 77 *Brackets for a roller blind*

(1) Cut the wooden roller to the correct size to fit between the two brackets.

(2) Cut the fabric to the exact size of the roller. If hems need to be made at each side a 2.5 cm (1 in) allowance must be made for these. The fabric should be approximately 15 cm (6 in) longer than the measurement of the window. This allows for turnings at the bottom edge of the blind and also enables fabric to be rolled round the roller when it is pulled down. It is very important to cut the fabric accurately otherwise the blind will not roll evenly. Square up the fabric with the edge of a table or use a T-square to get accurate angles.

Fig. 78 *Making a casing at the lower edge of the blind*

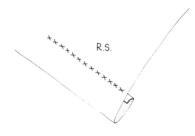

R.S.

Fig. 79 *Positioning the blind to the roller*

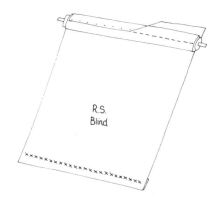

R.S.
Blind

Making the roller blind

Decide whether the blind is to be fixed inside or outside the window recess (*fig. 76*). If a kit cannot be obtained in the exact size buy the next size up and trim the roller down to the size required.

A kit consists of a wooden roller which has a spring and metal cap with a rectangular pin at one end of the roller. Another metal end cap with a round pin is provided to fit onto the other end of the roller when it has been cut to the exact size required. Two metal brackets are supplied; one is fixed to the left hand side of the window to take the sprung end and rectangular pin, and the other bracket is fixed at the right hand side of the window and takes the end with the round pin (*fig. 77*). Follow the manufacturer's instructions for fixing these. Special tacks are also provided for applying the fabric to the roller. An acorn fitment with tacks and a pull cord is also provided, together with a wooden batten to give weight to the bottom hem of the blind.

46

2 *This well-proportioned pelmet conceals the curtain tracks and headings, and the tasselled tie-backs hold the curtains to give maximum light*

(3) At the lower edge turn up 1.3 cm (½ in) to the wrong side of the blind and then turn over 3.8 cm (1½ in) to make a casing for the wooden batten. Use a little adhesive to hold the hem in place and then machine along the hem using a zig zag stitch (*fig. 78*).

(4) Position the blind to the roller as in fig. 79, making sure that the right side is uppermost. Place the fabric to the guide line on the roller and stick down with a little adhesive. Tack down every 3.8 cm (1½ in) along the roller.

(5) Cut the wooden batten to the width of the blind and insert in the casing at the lower edge. Knot one end of the pull cord and thread through the acorn fitting. Screw the fitment to the wrong side of the blind.

(6) The lower edge of the blind can be decorated with braid, or a piece of blind fabric can be cut to the shape chosen and fixed to the back of the casing with adhesive (*fig. 80*).

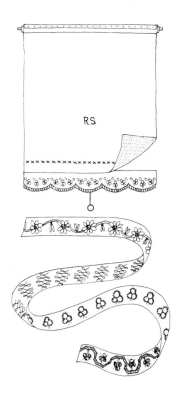

Fig. 80 *Applying a trimming to the lower edge of a blind*

6
PELMETS AND VALANCES

Pelmets

Pelmets came into fashion in about the seventeenth century and were developed from the valance because of architectural changes in window design. Originally a pelmet was an embroidered strip of fabric, but it later developed into something very elaborate and ornate, and was used well into the Victorian era. In recent years the trend has been away from pelmets and valances, but in fact well designed pelmets or valances can add considerably to the interest and originality of a room's decor. They create a decorative finish to the tops of curtains and at the same time conceal tracks and heading.

When designing a pelmet, care should be taken to make it proportionate to the height of the room and the window.

A simple design can be as effective as a more elaborate one, and sometimes the pattern of the fabric can suggest a suitable design for the pelmet. Alternatively, try using a design from a chair in the room if it belongs to an interesting period (*fig. 81*).

Pelmets give a look of distinction to a room and are most effective when used with roller blinds. They are also very successful when draping dressing tables and beds.

A pelmet is usually made to match the curtains and is mounted on a special buckram foundation. Pelmet buckram is a coarse canvas impregnated with glue. It is sold by the metre in narrow widths, so joins do not need to be made to obtain the required length.

A stiffened pelmet should be fixed to a pelmet board and not on to a valance rail. Pelmet boards should be approximately 10 cm (4 in) deep by 16 mm ($\frac{5}{8}$ in), 2.5 cm (1 in) thick and should extend 5–7.5 cm (2–3 in) beyond the end of the curtain track. They are fixed like a shelf, using brackets. The height of fixing above the window frame can be varied to suit the effect required. For an average window the board is fixed approximately 5–7.5 cm (2–3 in) above the frame. The pelmet is than attached to the front edge of the board with drawing pins or Velcro.

Pelmets made with buckram cannot be washed and must be dry cleaned, but regular brushing or vacuuming should keep them in good condition.

Estimating the fabric

Measure the length of the pelmet board from wall to wall, remembering to include the 10 cm (4 in) return at each end. To this measurement add 5 cm (2 in) for turnings. The depth of the pelmet is determined by the design (allow 3.8 cm (1½ in) pelmet to 30.5 cm (12 in) of curtain drop, or one sixth of the total depth of floor length curtains). To this measurement add 10 cm (4 in) for turnings. In rooms with low ceilings keep the depth of the pelmet to a minimum, but not usually less than 18 cm (7 in).

Centre the width of the fabric in the middle of the pelmet and add any extra fabric to each side of this width. Never have a seam at the centre of the pelmet. When estimating the amount of fabric required, remember to

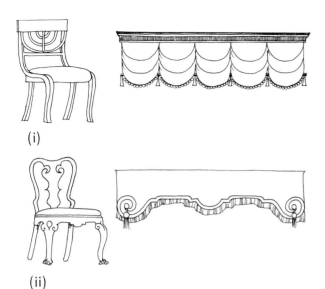

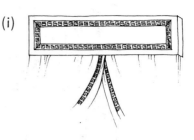

(i)

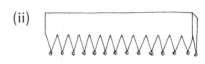

(ii)

(iii)

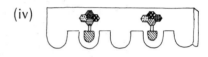

(iv)

(v)

(vi)

(i)

(ii)

Fig. 81 *Period styles reflect pelmet design*
- *(i) Regency*
- *(ii) Georgian*

allow for pattern matching. The same amount of lining sateen and interlining is needed as for the face fabric. Interlining gives more body to the fabric, and a slightly padded look to the pelmet.

Making the pelmet
(1) Make a template of the design required using stiff paper or newspaper. When a satisfactory design has been achieved fold the template in half and cut the other side to match. The design is then ready to transfer to the pelmet buckram.

Fig. 82 *Some ideas for pelmet designs*
- *(i) Decorative braid*
- *(ii) Pavilion edge design*
- *(iii) Covered buttons used to trim the pelmet*
- *(iv) Use of patchwork*
- *(v) Use braid*
- *(vi) Contrasting piping used to outline the design*
- *(vii) Quilting used as surface decoration*

(vii)

50

(2) Cut a strip of buckram the exact length of the pelmet board (including the 10 cm (4 in) returns at each end). If it is necessary to join the buckram, overlap the two edges 1.3 cm (½ in) and machine into position.

(3) Lay the template on the buckram and secure it by damping the buckram very slightly and ironing the paper pattern to it. Cut out the buckram, using a sharp pair of scissors.

(4) Cut a strip of fabric 10 cm (4 in) larger all round than the exact size of the finished pelmet. This allows for the fabric to be turned over onto the buckram (*fig. 83*). Join widths of fabric where necessary, keeping a full width of fabric at the centre of the pelmet. Make 1.3 cm (½ in) seams, matching patterns carefully (*figs. 11 and 12*). Press seams open.

(5) Cut a strip of bump or domette 5 cm (2 in) larger than the exact size of the finished pelmet, joining the pieces with a lapped seam and two rows of zigzag machine stitching. Place the buckram onto the interlining, exactly in the centre. Starting at the top edge of the pelmet dampen the buckram at the edges with a small cloth. Fold over the interlining and press firmly to the buckram with a hot iron. Continue in this way all round the pelmet, slashing curves and cutting away surplus fabric on the con-

vex curves. Right-angled curves also need slashing and the surplus fabric trimmed away.

(6) Lay the buckram and the interlining on to the wrong side of the face fabric and tack into position along the top edge making sure that the fabric is correctly positioned on the right side. Fold over the face fabric on to the wrong side of the buckram (*fig. 83*). Dampen the buckram and press down in the same way as for the interlining, slashing curves and mitring each corner (*fig. 84*). If the fabric frays easily, reinforce each slash with a few buttonhole stitches.

(7) If decorative trimming, braid or piping is used, this should be stitched to the pelmet before the lining is applied. With the right side of the pelmet facing, stab stitch the trimming to the pelmet using matching thread (*fig. 84*).

(8) Cut a strip of lining sateen 5 cm (2 in) larger than the finished pelmet. Join strips together, if necessary, with 1.3 cm (½ in) turnings and press seams open. With the wrong side of the pelmet facing, turn in the lining 1.3 cm (½ in) and pin 6 mm (¼ in) from the top edge of the pelmet. Turn in the sides in the same way. Cut the lining to the shaped edge allowing 2.5 cm (1 in) for turnings and turn in as before, slashing where necessary. Slipstitch the lining to the pelmet all round (*fig. 85*).

(9) Cut a piece of heading tape 2.5–3.8 cm (1–1½ in) wide the length of the pelmet plus 2.5 cm (1 in) for turnings. Pin the tape to the top edge of the pelmet and turn in 1.3 cm (½ in) at each end. Using matching buttonhole thread, back stitch the ends and lower edge of the tape to the pelmet, making sure that the stitches go through to the buckram but not to the face fabric. Stitch the tape down every 9–10 cm (3½–4 in) to form pockets (*fig. 85*) and attach to the pelmet board with drawing pins.

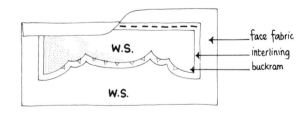

Fig. 83 *Turning the fabric on to the buckram*

(10) Alternatively, a piece of Velcro can be stitched to the back of the pelmet and the matching strip glued to the front of the pelmet board.

(11) Buttons can be covered in the face fabric and applied to the right side of the pelmet for decoration. Alternatively, motifs of patchwork or other decorative embroidery could be used.

Valances

A valance is a piece of gathered or pleated fabric used where a soft informal effect is required. Valances are shortened versions of curtains, and any of the commercial heading tapes can be used to make them (*fig. 86*). Estimate the amount of fabric required as for curtains (see Chapter 5). The depth of the valance should be calculated in the same way as for a stiffened pelmet, i.e. 3.8 cm (1½ in) of valance per 30.5 cm (12 in) of curtain drop.

Valances are not usually stiffened with buckram, but they can be interlined with bump or a non-woven interfacing when thinner fabrics are used. They should always be

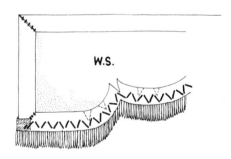

Fig. 84 *Trimming applied to the pelmet with stab stitch*

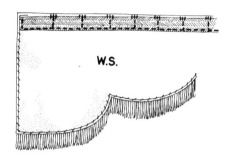

Fig. 85 *Heading tape applied to the wrong side of the pelmet*

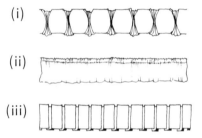

Fig. 86 *Valances are hung like curtains – on hooks from a separate rail*
(i) Pinch pleated
(ii) Gathered
(iii) Box pleated

lined. The back of the valance should be finished with a curtain heading tape and either hung from a valance rail or attached to a pelmet board with drawing pins or Velcro. The tape should be attached 3.8–5 cm (1½–2 in) from the top of the back of the valance so that it covers the top of the rail or board. This also prevents it from sagging.

Valances can be used round dressing tables, vanitory units and baths. They are also effective when making bed canopies and drapes for tester and half-tester beds.

3 *A feminine look for a bedroom is created by the use of bed drapes and frilled cushions*

7

CUSHIONS AND LOOSE COVERS

Cushions can be made in all shapes and sizes, and from almost any type of fabric. They often add the finishing touch to a room by providing impact or individuality. A cushion can be decorated, for example, with patchwork, quilting, embroidery, lace, frills, piping or contrasting borders to give originality. Cushions are costly accessories to buy, but they can be made easily and inexpensively from remnants of fabrics left over from home sewing projects.

A cushion must be comfortable as well as decorative, and in this respect it is only as good as its filling. A good foundation is essential for a successful cushion and the right sort of filling should be chosen for each cushion according to its function.

As well as being decorative, cushions are often used to provide extra seating and they can be made most successfully for window seats, kitchen benches, gardens, bathrooms and so on. Large floor cushions and sag bags are useful forms of seating for children's and teenagers' rooms (see Chapter 8). Special

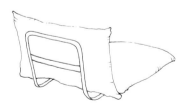

Fig. 87 *Tubular frame used to keep back and seat cushions in position*

tubular cushion frames can be obtained from some stores to keep large back and seat cushions in place, and these also provide useful seating for both the garden and the home (*fig. 87*).

When sewing for the garden and out of doors choose tough, practical fabrics such as deckchair canvas, sailcloth, p.v.c. and heavyweight cottons. Remember to use fillings for cushions that do not absorb moisture. Furnishings in the garden should enhance and not compete with nature, so choose bold bright colours in plains, stripes, checks and geometric shapes. These provide more impact out of doors than printed fabrics with small flowery patterns.

Fillings for Cushions

Down
This is an expensive filling which is very light in weight. It is soft and resilient and holds its shape well. It is a good choice for cushions made from fine fabrics. About ½ kg (1 lb) down is needed to make a cushion approximately 51 x 51 cm (20 x 20 in). Use downproof cambric for making an inner cover so that the down does not work through the weave of the fabric.

Feathers
These are much cheaper than pure down but are heavy when used on their own, so they are often mixed with down to make cushions lighter in weight. Featherproof ticking or downproof cambric should be used for the

inner cover. If black and white striped ticking is used make sure that it will not show through the cushion cover fabric. About 1 kg (2 lb) feathers are needed for a cushion 51 x 51 cm (20 x 20 in).

Kapok

This is a vegetable fibre which is light in weight and inexpensive. It is non-absorbent so is suitable for garden cushions, but it goes lumpy after a few years' wear. About 500 g (1 lb) kapok is sufficient to fill a small cushion 38—45.5 cm (15—18 in) square. Use calico or sheeting for the inner cover.

Synthetic wadding

Wadding made from man-made fibres, such as Terylene, Dacron and Courtelle, is inexpensive and non-absorbent. This filling is washable and will not work through the inner cover. To make a cushion fully washable, both the inner and the outer covers should be made in washable fabrics.

Latex and plastic foam

This can be obtained in blocks of various shapes, sizes, thicknesses and qualities and can be cut with a very sharp knife. It keeps its shape well. It should be covered with a calico or strong cotton inner cover to protect it, as it is affected by light and heat and tends to crumble with wear.

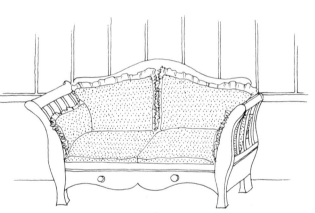

Fig. 89 *Loose cushions used effectively*

Fig. 88 *Some styles for cushions*

Plastic foam chips

These can be used as an inexpensive filling for cushion pads, but they do not have the same smooth appearance as other fillings. They are suitable for gardens and children's rooms as they do not absorb moisture.

Polystyrene granules

These are tiny expanded polystyrene beads

55

which are used for making sag bags. They can also be used for making beds for dogs and cats and are washable (*fig. 122*). Use a strong calico or cotton fabric for the inner cover.

Making Basic Cushion Shapes

Cushions can be made in all shapes. Square cushions vary in size from 38 cm (15 in) upwards, depending on the purpose for which they are required. Round cushions can be made to any size, with or without a boxed edge, and can be made to fit stools or chairs with or without ties. Variations can be made by cutting out shapes in triangles, diamonds, hearts or shells (*fig. 88*). Always make a paper pattern first before cutting out the material, remembering that the filling will take up some of the fabric. Cut the pattern slightly larger to allow for this.

Delicate fabrics lend themselves to decorative edges such as frills and pleating, whereas heavier furnishing fabrics are best self-piped with fabric in a contrasting colour.

Making the Pad

To make a well-filled, plump cushion, make the inner pad 1.3 cm (½ in) larger all round than the outer cushion cushion cover. For example, for a 38 cm square (15 in) cushion the finished inner pad should measure 40.5 m (16 in). This applies only when making cushions with loose fillings such as down, feather, kapok etc. For a latex or plastic foam shape the inner cover must be made to the exact size, as this filling is rigid and firm.

Cut two pieces of fabric the size required allowing 1.3 cm (½ in) turnings for seams. Place the right sides together and machine round the four sides leaving an opening of approximately 20.5 cm (8 in) on one side. When using downproof cambric use a fine needle and two rows of machine stitching. Wax along the stitching with a piece of beeswax to prevent the filling working through the holes made by the machine needle. Clip

at corners and turn the cover to the right side and fill. Sew up the opening with oversewing stitches and wax if necessary.

Openings

All cushion covers need an opening, but this does not necessarily need to be permanent. A neat finish can be obtained by slipstitching the opening together when the pad has been inserted, and this can be done on all cushions that are purely decorative. However, if a cushion cover needs to be removed regularly for washing or cleaning it needs to have a more permanent opening.

Leave an opening large enough to enable the pad to be inserted easily, making it to come within 2.5 cm (1 in) of the two corners on one side. Position the opening so that it shows as little as possible when the cushion is finished, having it at the back of the cushion or at the bottom edge where possible.

Where a permanent opening is necessary, choose from the following:

1. Zip fasteners

Zip fasteners make a neat finish, but make sure that a long enough zip is used so that there is no undue strain on it when the cushion pad is removed. The zip should be 5 cm (2 in) shorter than the side of the cushion where it is being inserted. Position the zip along the piped edge of the cushion cover in the seam where possible, as this is less conspicuous than having it at the centre back. However, if a very thick fabric is being used, or the cushion cover has a definite back and front (e.g. canvas work or embroidery), the zip can be positioned at the centre back.

For example:

(a) Cut out the front of the cushion cover 40.5 x 40.5 cm (16 x 16 in). For the back cut two pieces 40.5 x 23 cm (16 x 9 in). This allows 2.5 cm (1 in) on each section for the seam across the back of the cushion cover (*fig. 90*).

(b) With right sides together pin and tack

56

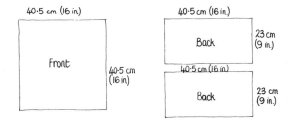

Fig. 90 *Cutting out a cushion cover*

the two back sections as in fig. 91. Machine stitch.

(c) Insert the zip in the opening (*fig. 92*) and leave partly unzipped. Zips can be inserted by machine using the zipper foot, or stitched by hand using a small back stitch. With right sides together pin and tack the front section of the cushion to the back section of the cushion. Machine all round. Clip corners and neaten edges (*fig. 93*). Open the zip completely and turn to the right side.

When applying a zip fastener to a piped opening use the following method:

(a) Open the zip and pin and tack the piped edge to one side of the zip, right sides together. Tack 3 mm ($\frac{1}{8}$ in) from the teeth of the zip (*fig. 94*). Machine or stitch by hand.

(b) Close the zip and pin and tack the other side of the zip to the 1.3 cm (½ in) turnings, making sure that the fold covers the teeth of the zip. Machine or stitch by hand 3 mm ($\frac{1}{8}$ in) from the teeth.

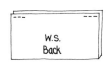

Fig. 91 *The two back sections stitched together leaving an opening for the zip fastener*

2. Velcro

Velcro is a 'touch and close' fastening which is made from two tapes with different surfaces. One is covered with a nylon fuzz and the other with tiny nylon hooks which catch onto the fuzz when the two surfaces are pressed together. To open, peel the two surfaces apart. A strip of each surface is sewn onto each side of the opening on the seam allowance. It washes and dry cleans well.

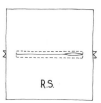

Fig. 92 *Zip fastener left partly unzipped*

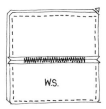

Fig. 93 *Corners clipped on the cushion cover*

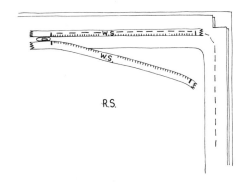

Fig. 94 *Zip fastener tacked to the piped edge of the cushion cover*

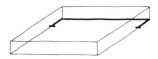

Fig. 95 *Box cushion showing position of opening*

3. Continuous wrap opening

This is a strong inconspicuous opening suitable for box cushion covers. The opening should be extended 5–10 cm (2–4 in) at each side edge (*fig. 95*). It can also be used for openings on loose covers.

(a)   Cut a length of fabric twice the length of the opening plus 2.5 cm (1 in). The width of the strip should be 6.4–7.5 cm (2½–3 in). Join the strip at the short sides with 1.3 cm (½ in) turnings.

(b)   Pin the right side of the strip to the right side of the cushion cover opening taking 1.3 cm (½ in) turnings. Tack and machine.

(c)   Along the unpiped edge of the opening cut away 1.3 cm (½ in) of fabric from the strip. Turn down 1.3 cm (½ in) along this cut-away side and fold over to the wrong side and hem stitch into position.

(d)   On the piped side of the opening turn over the strip 1.3 cm (½ in) and fold over onto the line of machine stitching. Stitch across firmly on fold at both ends of the opening (*fig. 96*). Apply hooks and bars and snap fasteners alternately along the opening.

Making the Cover

These are some of the methods of making cushion covers for basic shapes using different techniques. Once these have been mastered many adaptations can be made to other shapes and sizes.

1. Square piped cushion

(a)   Cut out two pieces of fabric the size of the cushion plus 1.3 cm (½ in) turnings on all sides. If the fabric frays easily

or is loosely woven allow 1.9 cm (¾ in). Make sure any motif is centralized.

(b)   Prepare enough crossway strip to go round the four sides of the cushion plus a little extra. Use the quick method described in Chapter 4.

(c)   Tack the crossway strip and the piping cord to the right side of the front section of the cover, tacking close to the piping cord. Machine the piping cord into position along the one edge where the opening will be, using a zipper foot.

(d)   Pin and tack the back section of the cover to the front section with right sides together, leaving the opening edge untacked. Machine into position using a zipper foot.

(e)   Clip the corners and neaten the seams with a zigzag machine stitch. Turn the cover to the right side and insert the cushion pad. Slipstitch the opening together or use a zip fastener as above.

2. Round squab cushion

(a)   Make a paper pattern the size of the cushion required. Use a round tray or a large plate to ensure a perfect circle. From the pattern cut two circles for the top and bottom sections of the cushion cover, allowing 1.3 cm (½ in) turnings all round. Cut a strip of fabric on the straight grain from selvedge to selvedge

Fig. 96 *Stitching across the end of the opening on the wrong side*

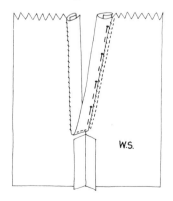

W.S.

for the welt. This should be cut to the required depth plus 1.3 cm (½ in) turnings on each edge and the length must be the circumference of the circle plus 7.5 cm (3 in) for the seam allowance and easing.

(b) Prepare enough crossway strip 3.8 cm (1½ in) wide for piping round the top and bottom sections of the cover plus a little extra. Apply the crossway strip and piping cord by pinning and tacking to the top and bottom sections of the cover, clipping at intervals to allow the piping to mould to the curve (*fig. 58*). Machine.

(c) Pin and tack the welt to the top section of the cover, right sides together, and find the exact position for the join in the welt. Tack and stitch this join. Machine stitch the welt into position uisng a zipper foot, keeping the stitching as close as possible to the piping cord (*fig. 97*).

(d) To make ties, cut 3.2 cm (1¼ in) wide strips of fabric on the straight grain long enough to make two ties — about 61 cm (24 in). Fold in half lengthwise and press. Machine all round. Mark positions for the ties on the bottom section of the cover and apply as in fig. 98 to the right side.

(e) Pin and tack the welt to the bottom section of the cushion cover taking care to match the warp and weft grain to the top section of the cover. Leave an opening at the back edge. This should measure approximately one-third of the circumference of the cushion. Machine seam. Neaten the raw edges and insert the cushion pad into the cover and slip stitch the opening together. (If a zip is used on a round cushion it is best to insert it down the back of the cushion, in which case the bottom section must be cut in two pieces and an allowance made for the seam as in the example in figs. 90–93.)

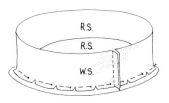

Fig. 97 *Making the join in the welt*

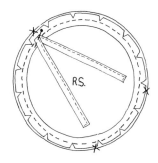

Fig. 98 *Positions for ties marked with an X*

3. Bolster cushions
These are long cushions often used on beds and divans. Covers can be made in combinations of fabrics with various edge finishes. Avoid using fabrics with large patterns as these may be difficult to match at the seams.

Bolster cushion with piped ends

(a) Cut two circles the size required allowing 1.3 cm (½ in) turnings all round. These circular ends should be cut from a paper pattern. Use a large plate or tray to make the pattern.

(b) Cut a rectangle of fabric on the straight grain, the circumference plus 2.5 cm (1 in) for turnings, and the required length of the cushion cover.

(c) With right sides together pin, tack and machine at each end of the long sides of the rectangle, leaving an opening at the centre (*fig. 99*). A zip fastener can be inserted in the opening or this can be slip stitched together when the pad has been inserted.

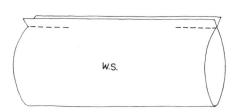

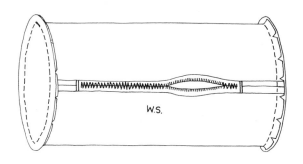

Fig. 99 *Stitching the rectangle, leaving an opening at the centre*

Fig. 100 *Stitching the circular ends to the tube*

(d) Apply crossway strip and piping cord to the two circular ends clipping the crossway to enable it to mould to the shape of the curve (*fig. 58*). Alternatively, a frill could be made and applied instead of piping.

(e) Pin and tack the circular ends to the tube with right sides together, snipping the seam allowance at intervals (*fig. 100*). Machine using a zipper foot, stitching as close as possible to the piping cord. Turn the cushion cover to the right side through the opening. Neaten the raw edges and insert the pad. Slip stitch the opening together.

Bolster cushion with gathered ends
A gathered end can be made for a bolster cushion by cutting a strip of fabric on the straight grain as long as the circumference of the circle plus 2.5 cm (1 in) and as wide as its radius. Join the short ends of the strip together and tack one long edge to the tube. Run a gathering stitch 1.3 cm (½ in) from the inner edge of the circle and draw up tightly to fit the centre of the circle. Fasten off ends securely. To neaten the centre sew a covered button or tassel over the raw edges at each end of the cushion cover (*fig. 101*).

4. Buttoning a cushion
Covered buttons can be used on many types of cushion covers and make an attractive decorative feature. Commercial moulds can be obtained in many sizes. To cover a button mould cut a piece of fabric 1.3 cm (½ in)

larger than the button mould. Make a running stitch round the edge of the fabric and draw up to fit over the mould.

To button down a cushion first mark the positions for the buttons on both sides of the cushion. Using double button thread and a long darning needle secure thread to the back of one button in the position marked. Take the thread through to the other side of the cushion cover to the point marked and into the back of the second button. Take the thread back to the first button and pull tightly so that the buttons sink into the cover. Knot and fasten off securely.

5. Loose cover for a chair
Loose covers can be made for many styles of chairs and sofas, as well as for divans, stools and pouffes. They can considerably extend the life of an upholstered chair by protecting it from dirt and dust.

Fig. 101 *Bolster cushion with gathered ends*

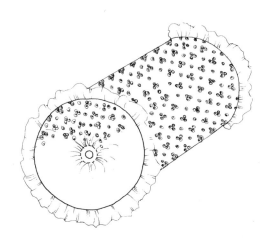

A collection of accessories for the nursery made in fabrics that go well together

It is essential to choose the right type of fabric before making loose covers, otherwise much time and effort will be wasted. The fabric should be sufficiently hardwearing to withstand regular laundering or dry cleaning and it should be shrink and fade resistant. Choose fabric that is firm, smooth and closely woven. Loosely woven material is not suitable as it loses its shape and wears out quickly. Use linen union, closely woven furnishing cotton, twill or lightweight upholstery fabrics for the best results. Do not use fabric that is too thick as this will be difficult to work when several layers of fabric are being sewn together.

An all-over design or random match pattern is easier to handle and more economical to use than a large pattern repeat, which may have motifs that need to be centralized on some sections of the cover and which will necessitate some wastage. If it is available use 78.5 cm (31 in) wide fabric, as this cuts more economically on small chairs than 122 cm (48 in) wide fabric.

Buy the best quality fabric possible and always be generous when estimating the amount needed. Spare fabric can be used for making extra arm caps and cushion covers, which extend the life of a loose cover.

Piping

All seams that define the outline of the chair should be piped. As well as strengthening the

Fig. 102 *Some styles for loose covers*

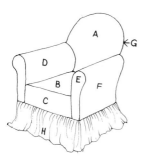

Fig. 103 *Sections of a loose cover*
A — Inside back
B — Seat
C — Front border
D — Inside arm
E — Front panel
F — Outside arm
G — Outside back

seams, this gives a professional finish to the cover. The fabric used for piping can be of a contrasting colour, but it should be similar in weight and texture to that of the loose cover fabric. Contrasting piping provides an effective decorative feature.

Tuck-Away

This is the fabric that is tucked in at the back and sides of the chair seat to hold the cover firmly in position. 15—20.5 cm (6—8 in) is normally allowed for this. It is important to make this allowance otherwise the cover will slip out of place with the constant use of the chair.

Measuring and Estimating

A quick estimate of the amount of fabric needed for a loose cover can be obtained by measuring five times the height of the back of the chair. However, before buying the fabric a more accurate estimate will be necessary. The following measurements should be taken with a fabric tape measure to find the total amount of fabric required. (The names of each section of a loose cover are given in fig. 103.)

(a) The bottom of the outside back to the top of the back, down the inside back to seat, plus 20.5 cm (8 in) for tuck-away and turnings.

(b) The back of the seat to the front of the seat down to the bottom of the front border, plus 20.5 cm (8 in) for tuck-away and turnings.

(c) The bottom of the outside arm, over the arm and down to the inside arm to the seat, plus 20.5 cm (8 in) for tuck-away and turnings. Double this measurement to allow for the two arms (*fig. 104*).

Add these three measurements together to obtain the amount of 78.5 cm (31 in) wide fabric needed. If using 122 cm (48 in) wide fabric, allow two-thirds of this amount.

To this total must be added 75 cm—1 m (1 yd) for making the crossway strip to cover the piping cord. If a frill or skirt is being made for the bottom edge an extra 1.5—3 m (1½—3 yd) must be allowed, depending on the style of frill chosen. An allowance of approximately 1 m (1 yd) should also be made for each loose cushion, and 1 m (1 yd) for each arm cap.

Each chair needs to be measured and planned individually. However, the approximate amount of 78.5 cm (31 in) wide fabric needed for making a cover for the average chair is 6.5—7 m (7 yd). This assumes a plain or textured fabric; more is needed if a pattern fabric is used. An allowance of at least one pattern repeat must be made for centralizing and matching patterns.

Fig. 104 *Taking measurements for a loose cover on a chair with a fixed edge*

Making the Chair Cover

A loose cover should always be cut on the chair. Never use a paper pattern (except for wings and small panels) and do not be tempted to unpick an old cover and use it as a pattern. It will almost certainly have stretched or shrunk and lost its original shape.

Make sure the chair is clean and the structure sound. The fabric is fitted on to one half of the chair only, using double fabric, so that when cut out both sides are identical. Find the centre of the chair by measuring with a fabric tape measure and mark down the centre of the outside back, inside back and along the centre of the seat and down the front border. Use tailor's chalk or pins.

Make small identification labels to attach to each section as it is cut out.

When cutting out each section, make sure that the straight of the grain runs to the floor, and mark this with tailor's chalk on the wrong side of the fabric when it has been cut. A chair is not always upright and may be slightly tilted; this point must be carefully checked.

(1) With right sides outside, so that the pattern, if any, can be seen, fold the fabric in half lengthwise. Place the fold to the centre line on the inside back of the chair (*fig. 105*). Sufficient fabric must project beyond the top of the chair to allow for 5 cm (2 in) turnings. If the fabric is patterned, make sure any motif is centralized. Allow 15–20.5 cm (6–8 in) for tuck-away at the lower edge of the inside back section. Cut off fabric. Upholstery pins or skewers can be used to hold the fabric to the chair while each section is cut (*fig. 108*).

(2) Place the folded fabric on to the seat in the same way, allowing 15–20.5 cm (6–8 in) for tuck-away at the back and 5 cm (2 in) for turnings at the front. Cut out.

(3) Cut out the front border in the same way, allowing 5 cm (2 in) for turnings if a frill or skirt is being applied to the bottom edge of the cover. Approximately 18 cm (7 in) should be allowed if the cover is to tie underneath the chair without a frill (*see fig. 117*).

(4) The outside back is cut in the same way, allowing 5 cm (2 in) at the lower edge if a frill or skirt is being made and 18 cm (7 in) for a tie-under finish.

(5) With the right sides outside, join the outside back at the top edge of the chair using a continuous line of pins. Pin the lower edge of the inside back to the seat, and pin the front of the seat to the front border.

(6) Cut the inside and outside arms separately, using single pieces of fabric and centralizing any pattern. You must allow 5 cm (2 in) turnings at the front to join with the front panel and at the back to join with the inside back. You must also allow 5 cm (2 in) turnings at the top of the inside and outside arms.

(7) The front panels must also be cut out separately using single fabric and, if patterned material is being used, making sure that a suitable motif is placed on each front panel so that they both match.

When all these pieces have been cut out, unpin all the sections. Make a lengthwise chalk line down the true grain of the fabric on the wrong side of each section. This serves as a guide to prevent the sections being pulled off grain when the cover is being fitted.

Check that an indentifying label is attached to each section.

Fitting the Cover

(1) Position all the sections and pin together on the chair with the right sides inside checking that the grain is positioned correctly. Follow the lines of the chair when pinning so that the seams that are to be piped define this line when the cover is completed (*fig. 106*).

Fig. 105 *Cutting out the fabric on the chair*

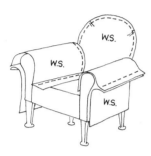

W.S.

W.S.

W.S.

Fig. 106 *Pinning the sections together with the right sides inside*

(2) When there is a fixed edge to a chair, that is, one with an unsprung edge (*fig. 104*), the tuck-away seams must be carefully tapered from nothing at the front border to 15–20.5 cm (6–8 in) at the back of the seat. However, if there is an independent edge to the chair (one which has a sprung edge, as in fig. 107) the loose cover must fit down into this 'V' where the front border joins up with the front panel. This is to allow the springs to work independently. If this is not done the fabric will tear after a short time because of the constant movement of the springs.

(3) Take in any excess fullness on the inside back by making small darts where necessary.

(4) When the cover is satisfactorily pinned, trim off any surplus fabric to leave 2.5 cm (1 in) turnings. Snip curves where necessary.

(5) Check pin lines again and adjust until a perfect fit is obtained. Make sure that the pins are firmly placed in the fabric.

(6) Remove the cover and tack the tuck-away seams and any darts that have been made.

Piping

Prepare about 10 m (10 yd) of No. 2 or 3 piping cord and cover with crossway strip (see Chapter 4). Pre-shrink the piping cord by boiling for five minutes and drying thoroughly before use.

Always apply the piping to the section of the loose cover that takes the shape of the chair, i.e. the outside back, the outside arms, the front border and the front panels, clipping crossway round curves. These sections fit well and do not need darts. The other sections that are applied to them are ones that sometimes need to be eased or darted to make them fit well.

Fig. 107 *Chair with an independent edge*

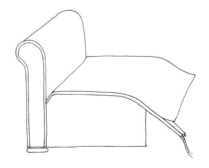

Fig. 108 *Upholstery pins and skewer*

(1) Remove a few pins at a time and apply the piping cord and crossway along the top edge of the outside arms. Pin and tack, using small tacking stitches and matching thread. If worked in matching thread these tacking stitches do not need to be removed when the cover is complete. Re-pin carefully and tack the side seam together.

(2) Remove the pins carefully and apply the piping and crossway to the top edge of the front border in the same way. Re-pin and tack.

(3) Apply piping and crossway round the front panels in the same way except at the lower edges where they meet the front border. Re-pin and tack. It is sometimes easier to apply the piping to the front panels before fitting these sections on to the chair.

(4) Most chair covers need an opening at the back to enable the cover to be removed easily. Mark the position for this. Remove pins and apply piping and crossway to the outside back as far as the top of the opening. At this point cross over the piping and apply it to the outside arm so that the opening is as inconspicuous as possible when the cover is finished.

(5) Tack any remaining seams before fitting the cover on the chair, wrong sides outside. Make any final adjustments that may be necessary and then remove the cover from the chair.

Machining the Cover

(1) Machine any darts on the inside back. Machine the tuck-away seams, starting at the front border on one side and finishing at the front border on the other side.

(2) Machine stitch the piped seams in the following order: outside arms, front border, front panels, outside back as far as the opening. When machining a piped seam use a zipper foot if possible.

This ensures that the stitching is as close as possible to the piping cord. Where two piped seams meet, pull out the piping cord from one seam and cut off 2.5 cm (1 in). This makes the seam less bulky.

(3) For extra strength make another row of machine stitching 6 mm (¼ in) away from the first on all seams. Trim seams to 1.3 cm (½ in) and neaten the edges.

Frills and Skirts

A frill or a skirt is often attached to the bottom edge of the chair cover and this can be made in different styles to suit the individual chair. It makes an attractive finish to the chair and can be lined to give extra body if a lightweight fabric is being used.

Measuring and preparing a frill
Fit the cover on to the chair and mark the base line, i.e. the position for the piping and the frill. This line should be marked using tailor's chalk or a line of pins. Measure with a rigid rule the height from the floor where the piping cord will be positioned. Care must be taken to see that the base line is marked the same distance from the floor all round. Chairs are often lower at the back than at the front and this must be checked carefully.

The frill or skirt can vary in depth from 15–20.5 cm (6–8 in) according to the size and type of chair, and should finish 1.3 cm (½ in) from the floor. Allow 1.3 cm (½ in) turnings at the top of the frill and 3.8 cm (1½ in) for the bottom hem. The frill can be made in the following styles:

Gathered frill: This is a very attractive finish for a small chair where the fabric drapes well and is suitable for gathering. Allow one-and-a-half times the measurement round the base line.

Box-pleated skirt: This gives a more tailored finish but uses more fabric. For this allow three times the measurement round the base line.

Inverted corner pleats: This is a tailored finish

which uses much less fabric than a box-pleated skirt. Measure the base line and allow 40.5 cm (16 in) extra for each pleat, plus turning allowance.

Making the frill
Cut out and prepare the frill or skirt before applying it to the cover.
(1) Cut strips across the width of the fabric (i.e. from selvedge to selvedge) the required depth of the frill plus turnings. The length of the strip is determined by the style of the frill (see above). Make sure any patterns are matched and that the bottom of the pattern comes at the hem. If possible, position joins in pleats or at the sides or back of the chair.
(2) Tack and machine the strips together using 1.3 cm (½ in) turnings. Press seams open. Make a 1.3 cm (½ in) double machined hem along the lower edge.
(3) Pin and tack the piping and crossway along the base guide line.

Applying the frill to the cover
Gathered frill
(1) Divide and mark the strip into four and work two rows of gathering stitches 1.3 cm (½ in) from the top edge along each section. This makes the distribution of fullness easier.
(2) Divide the base line of the loose cover into four equal sections. Pin the frill to the cover, matching sections. Start pinning at the back opening at the outside arm and continue round the cover finishing at the outside back.
(3) Draw up the gathering threads to fit into each section on the cover. Adjust gathers and tack into position.
(4) Machine the frill to the cover, using a zipper foot and make two rows of machine stitching 6 mm (¼ in) apart. Neaten edges.

Box-pleated skirt
(1) Prepare the strips of fabric. Pleats can be formed in several ways, but equidistant

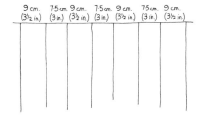

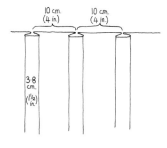

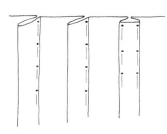

Figs. 109, 110 and 111 *Making box pleats*

box pleats are the most frequent choice. To make equidistant pleats, use figs. 109, 110 and 111 as a guide. The size of the pleats and spaces can be varied to suit individual requirements. Care should be taken when planning the pleating to make sure that a pleat is positioned at each corner of the front of the cover (*fig. 112*). Try to position any joins in the pleats, if possible, so that they do not show (*fig. 113*).

67

Fig. 112 *Positioning the pleats on a box pleated skirt*

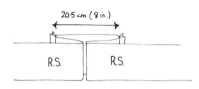

Fig. 113 *Making an inverted pleat showing joins positioned in pleat*

Fig. 114 *Inverted pleats positioned at each corner*

Fig. 115 *Slashing fabric at corners to make a tie-under finish*

(2) Pin the frill to the cover starting at the back opening. Begin with a space and continue pinning, arranging a pleat at each corner of the front of the cover. If possible, both ends of the front border should start with half a space. Alternatively, a pleat should be placed at each corner.

A little adjustment to the pleat may be necessary to achieve this arrangement, but it is important to make sure that the pleating is correct as it is in a very prominent position.

Skirt with inverted corner pleats

(1) Prepare the strips of fabric. Make an inverted pleat (a box pleat in reverse) for each corner of the cover and tack firmly into position.

(2) Pin the skirt to the cover, matching corner pleats to the corners of the cover (*fig. 114*). At the back opening arrange half an inverted pleat at each side of the opening.

(3) Tack and machine into position using a zipper foot and two rows of machine stitching. Neaten edges.

Tie-under finish

When a cover is finished without a frill or skirt it is necessary to tie it underneath the chair in order to hold it firmly in position. When cutting out the cover an allowance of 18 cm (7 in) must be made on the outside back, outside arms and the front border for a tie-under finish. This needs to be fitted round each chair leg, faced with bias binding, and a casing made for threading through the tape, which will then tie underneath the chair.

(1) Make a continuous wrap opening at the back of the chair (see page 58).

(2) With the cover on the chair, mark the position of the feet with tailor's chalk, allowing 1.3 cm (½ in) for turnings. Slash up at each leg, carefully fitting the fabric round the leg and cutting away the surplus fabric (*fig. 115*).

68

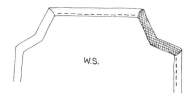

Fig. 116 *Tie-under finish. Cut away edges bound and hem made to form casing*

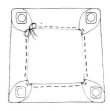

Fig. 117 *Tape threaded through casings and tied in position underneath the chair*

(3)   Remove the cover from the chair and face the cut away edges with bias binding or crossway strip made from matching fabric (*fig. 116*).

(4)   Make a 1.3 cm (½ in) hem at the bottom edge of the four flaps to form a casing for the tape. Thread a piece of strong tape through the four casings. Place the cover in position on the chair and draw up and tie the tapes firmly underneath the chair (*fig. 117*).

Openings for Loose Covers

Finish openings on loose covers with a continuous wrap using hooks and bars or Velcro to give added strength (*figs. 118 and 119*). A zip can be used, but choose one that is strong enough to take considerable strain. Except in the case of a tie-under finish the opening should be worked after the frill or skirt has been applied.

Wing Chairs

When making a cover for a wing chair the same techniques apply, but separate pieces should be cut for the front and back wing sections to make the cover fit well. A paper pattern can be made of these sections if necessary before cutting out the fabric. Allow 2.5 cm (1 in) for turnings and an allowance for a tuck-in if there is one. The inside of the wing may require darts, and these should be tacked and tried onto the chair before machining.

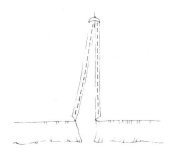

Fig. 118 *Making a continuous wrap opening on a loose cover*

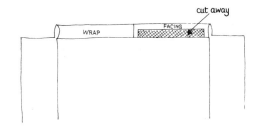

Fig. 119 *Trimming away facing to make a continuous wrap opening on a loose cover*

Sofas.

The same principles apply when measuring, cutting and making loose covers for sofas and all other upholstered chairs.

A loose cover for a sofa is treated in the same way as a chair, except that additional width is required to cover the two or three seats. Fabric should be carefully matched across the inside back of the sofa and motifs carefully centralized, but the pieces can be piped if necessary to divide the sections on the inside back. These seams should correspond with the edges of the seat cushions if there are any. When there are no seat cushions, the seat sections should correspond to the inside back sections (*fig. 120*).

Extra fabric will be needed for the outside back, inside back, seat, front border, and frill, as well as for any loose cushions. More piping

Fig. 120 *Seams on inside back correspond with seams on seat sections*

cord and crossway strip will also be needed, so a little extra fabric should be allowed for this.

If a sofa is to have a tie-under finish, it is best to sew two 20.5—25.5 (8—10 in) tapes to each flap and tie together behind each leg.

5 *Roller blind and cushions made in matching fabrics for the playroom*

8
CHILDREN'S ROOMS AND PLAYROOMS

In this chapter ideas will be given for making interesting and practical items for children's and teenagers, rooms, for nurseries and for playrooms. With a knowledge of the techniques described in previous chapters the items given will be easy to make and will certainly provide much pleasure. All of them are practical, and make ideal presents for children of all ages. Some can be made from fabrics left over from home sewing projects, and all will be economical.

Floor Cushions

These provide popular seating in children's and teenagers' rooms and are very simple to make. Use large bold patterns and colours for the best effects (*fig. 121*). Avoid using detachable trimmings, as these could be dangerous for very young children.

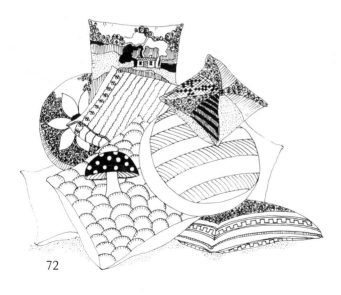

Floor cushion 91.5 x 91.5 cm (36 x 36 in) (approx.)

2 m (2 yd) fabric 122 cm (48 in) wide. Strong furnishing cotton, corduroy, denim or canvas for the outer cover.

2 m (2 yd) strong cotton or calico for the inner pad.

4 m (4 yd) piping cord (Nos. 3 or 4).

Plastic foam chips or synthetic wadding for the filling.

(1) Cut out two pieces of calico or strong cotton 94 x 94 cm (37 x 37 in) to make the inner pad. With right sides together, tack and machine round the four sides leaving an opening of approximately 30.5 cm (12 in) on one side through which to insert the filling.

(2) Clip the corners and turn to the right side. Fill with plastic foam chips or synthetic wadding and sew up the opening firmly with oversewing stitches.

(3) Measure the filled pad to find the finished measurement of the cushion cover. Cut the outer cover fabric to this size plus 1.3 cm (½ in) turnings. (If the fabric frays, allow 1.9—2.5 cm (¾—1 in) turnings.)

(4) Cut and prepare crossway strip to cover the piping using the quick method described in Chapter 4. Apply the crossway strip with the piping cord to the

Fig. 121 *Cushions for children's rooms using bold patterns and colours*

1 *Sophisticated use of complementary fabrics*

2 *The quilted bedspread complements the curtains and pelmet*

Fig. 122 *Cushions filled with polystyrene granules make comfortable beds for dogs*

right side of the top section of the cover, tacking close to the cord. Machine into position along the one side where the opening will be positioned.

(5) Pin and tack the bottom section of the cover to the top section with right sides together, leaving the opening edge untacked. Machine.

(6) Clip the corners and neaten the seams. Turn the cover to the right sides and insert the cushion pad. Sew up the opening firmly. Alternatively, insert a strong zip fastener as described in the previous chapter.

Sag Bags and Dog Cushions

Large squashy cushions that mould to the shape of the body make attractive seating for both adults and children (*fig. 123*). They are light to carry about and fun to use. Make them to co-ordinate with other soft furnishings or use strong denim, corduroy or canvas for teenagers' rooms. They are filled with expanded polystyrene beads and are very much cheaper to make than to buy ready made. Care must be taken when filling them to avoid spillage as the beads are difficult to handle. Smaller versions of the sag bag can be made for younger children. They also make comfortable beds for dogs (*fig. 122*).

Large sag bag
4.5 m (4½ yd) fabric for the outer cover. Use strong furnishing cotton, denim, canvas, corduroy, or use a co-ordinating mixture of two or three different fabrics. Preferably use fabric without a nap.

4.5 m (4½ yd) fabric for the inner lining. This should be reasonably strong, as it has to contain the polystyrene beads. Use heavyweight furnishing cotton, repp or calico.
Cardboard tube for filling the sag bag.
6—7 cu.m (8—9 cu.ft) expanded polystyrene beads.

(1) Draw a paper pattern using the measurements given in fig. 125 as a guide. Cut out two base sections and six side sections, in both the cover fabric and the inner lining fabric.

(2) Make the inner lining first. With right sides facing each other pin, tack and machine the two base sections together leaving a 15 cm (6 in) opening in the middle (*fig. 126*).

(3) With right sides facing pin and tack the long sides of the side sections together taking 1.3 cm (½ in) turnings to make a circular shape (*fig. 127*). Work two rows of machine stitching 3 mm ($\frac{1}{8}$ in) apart to give extra strength. Clip curves where necessary.

Fig. 123 *Sag bag decorated with patchwork motifs*

Fig. 124 *Smaller version of a sag bag with contrasting piping*

(4) With right sides facing pin and tack the base section into position, matching it to the six side sections (*fig. 128*). Machine into position, using two rows of stitching for extra strength, and turn to the right side.

(5) Make the outer cover in the same way as the lining but leaving a 30.5 cm (12 in) opening in the middle of the base section and insert a strong zip. Clip curves, neaten seams and turn the cover to the right side.

To fill the sag bag
(1) Make a cardboard tube approximately 6.4–7.5 cm (2½–3 in) in diameter and approximately 30.5–35.5 cm (12–14 in) long (or use one ready made).

(2) Insert the inner case into the outer cover so that the openings are at the base. Place on the floor. Insert the cardboard tube into the inner case opening and

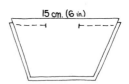

Fig. 126 *Sewing the two base sections together*

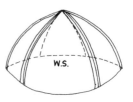

Fig. 127 *Side sections machine stitched into position*

Fig. 128 *Base sections matched to the six side sections*

secure it firmly to the opening with sticky tape. Make sure there are no gaps between the fabric and the cardboard or the beads will escape. Put the bag of polystyrene beads onto a chair. Make a hole in the bag, very carefully, and insert the other end of the tube. Secure the tube tightly with sticky tape and gently shake the beads down into the sag bag (*fig. 129*). Make sure that the tape is secure at all times during this process.

(3) When the sag bag is three-quarters full and all the beads are in the inner case, carefully secure the opening using double thread and small oversewing stitches.

Fig. 125 *Making a pattern for a sag bag*

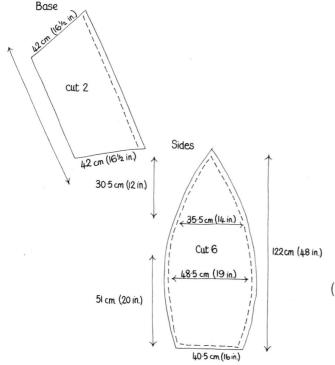

Base

42 cm (16½ in.)

cut 2

42 cm (16½ in.)

30·5 cm (12 in.)

Sides

35·5 cm (14 in.)

Cut 6

48·5 cm (19 in.)

122 cm (48 in.)

51 cm (20 in.)

40·5 cm (16 in.)

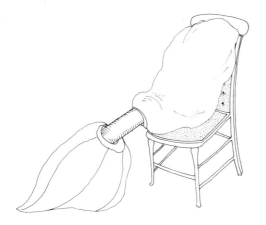

Fig. 129 *Filling the sag bag with the granules, using a cardboard tube*

(4) Shake the beads to distribute them in the bag and close the zip on the outer cover.

Smaller versions of the sag bag can be made for younger children by reducing the pattern slightly. Alternatively, make a pattern for a bolster cushion as in fig. 130. Follow the instructions for making up as in Chapter 7, inserting matching or contrasting piping. A smaller amount of beads would be needed to fill a smaller bag (approx. 3 cu. m, 4 cu. ft).

To make a dog or cat cushion, cut a round or oval paper pattern the size required: for a small dog, approximately 66 cm (26 in) x 56 cm (22 in); medium size, 91.5 cm (36 in) x 81.5 cm (32 in); large size, 112 cm (44 in) x 86.5 cm (34 in). Cut out and make up as for the round seat cushion (Chapter 7) inserting a 10 cm (4 in) welt. Omit the ties and the piping.

If the dog cushion is made in washable fabric, the whole cushion can be washed in soapy water. The water runs off the beads and so the cushion is not too heavy to handle. Rinse and drain well and hang outside to dry.

Fun Cushions and Pyjama Cases

Attractive fun cushions and pyjama cases can be made very successfully using animal, bird and fish motifs for inspiration. Patterns for these should be kept as simple as possible, and

rely on two main body sections only. The success of these cushions lies in the choice of fabric and of surface decoration. Paper patterns are available for these types of cushion, but it is more fun and much less expensive to make up designs of your own, using pictures and toys for guidance (*fig. 132*).

Cushions made in the usual way can be easily adapted to pyjama and nightdress cases by making an opening in the back section and inserting a zip fastener. To give the front of the case extra body, interline it with synthetic wadding or other interlining fabric.

Use coloured felts, rug wools, beads, sequins, buttons and ribbons for decorating such cushions and cases, and use simple embroidery techniques for making eyes, mouths, etc. and for outlining feet and paws. Make sure that any filling used is not inflammable, and that the trimmings are not easily detachable — which could be dangerous for young children.

Detailed instructions for making the lion pyjama case are given below. As long as simple designs are made, without the use of gussets, the same principle can be applied when making other shapes such as dogs, rabbits and teddy bears.

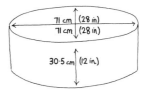

Fig. 130 *Measurements for a junior size sag bag*

Fig. 131 *Making a dog cushion*

75

Fig. 132 *Some ideas for fun cushions and pyjama cases*

Lion pyjama case
50 cm (18 in) 91.5 cm (36 in) wide fabric for the cover. Choose corduroy, felt, fur fabrics or strong cottons in bold colours.
Oddments of coloured felt for nose and eyes.
25.5 cm (10 in) zip fastener.
2.5 m (2½ yd) fringing 3.8 cm (1½ in)—5 cm (2 in) wide, or thick wool to make a fringing.
Synthetic wadding for interlining.
50 cm (18 in) cotton fabric for inner lining.
Stranded embroidery cotton.

(1) Make a paper pattern of a circle 35.5 cm (14 in) in diameter, using a tray or large plate as a guide. Cut two half circles for the back sections, plus 1.3 cm (½ in) turnings along the straight edge. Cut two circles 6.4 cm (2½ in) in diameter for the eyes, two smaller sections for the inner eye, and a triangle for the nose with 3.8 cm (1½ in) sides (*fig. 133*). From the patterns cut out the fabric, making sure the grain line is placed correctly. Cut out felt pieces for the eyes and nose.

(2) On the right side of the front section, position the nose and eye sections and pin in place. Make an outline for the mouth with a tacking line or tailor's chalk. Appliqué the nose and eye sections into position using herringbone or running stitch. Alternatively, apply these using a good adhesive (e.g. UHU).

(3) Using stranded embroidery cotton stitch the mouth with a simple embroidery stitch such as chain stitch (*fig. 135*) and work three French knots above it on each side of the nose (*fig. 134*).

(4) Pin and tack a double row of commercial fringing on the right side of the front section 1.3 cm (½ in) in from the raw edges. Overlap the ends and machine stitch into position (*fig. 134*). Alternatively, make a fringe by cutting a piece of thick paper 3.8—5 cm (1½—2 in) wide and 30.5—35.5 cm (12—14 in) long. Wind thick wool or rug wool round the strip of paper and machine along one long side 6 mm (¼ in) from the edge. Cut the wool along the other long side and remove the paper (*fig. 136*). Apply the fringing to the front section of the case as for the commercial fringing. (Approximately three of these lengths will be needed.)

(5) Using the paper pattern of the front section of the pyjama case cut a piece of synthetic wadding and a piece of lining cotton. Apply the wadding and

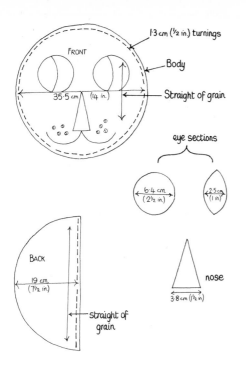

Fig. 133 *Pattern guide for lion pyjama case*

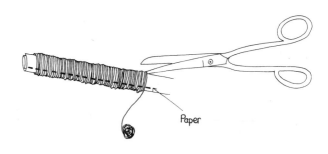

Fig. 136 *Making a handmade fringe from thick wool*

Fig. 134 *Nose and eye motifs appliquéd to the front section. Fringing stitched in position*

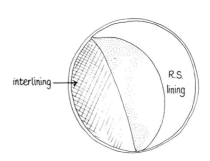

Fig. 137 *Wadding and lining applied to the front section of the pyjama case*

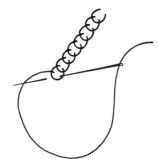

Fig. 135 *Chain stitch to outline the mouth*

the lining to the wrong side of the front section and pin and tack all round (*fig. 137*).

(6) With right sides together pin the back sections along the straight sides leaving a 25.5 cm (10 in) opening for the zip fastener. Machine and press seams open. Insert zip and open zipper.

(7) With right sides together, pin the front section of the pyjama case to the back section, having raw edges even. Tack and machine into position. Clip curves, neaten edges and turn right sides out (*fig. 138*).

If making a cushion, make an inner cushion pad first in the usual way (Chapter 7) and insert into the outer cover through the zip fastener opening. Omit the synthetic wadding and lining as in (5) above.

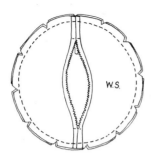

Fig. 138 *Front and back sections machine stitched into position*

Quilting — Carry Cot Cover

Quilting is an attractive form of surface decoration for cushion covers, bedspreads and many other items used in the home. It provides warmth as well as decoration and is therefore particularly suitable when making cot quilts and bedcovers or lining moses baskets.

Wadded quilting (also known as English quilting) was first introduced into Europe in the eleventh and twelfth centuries, and the craft developed and flourished in Wales and the northern counties of England. It was a means of holding three layers of fabric together to produce a warm covering for the bed. Sheep's wool was gathered from the hedgerows and was used for the padding between two layers of fabric. Nowadays synthetic wadding is generally used, as this is fully washable. However, bump and domette can be used, but these must be dry cleaned.

Originally simple geometric shapes were used in the designs for quilting, but as time went on templates and patterns were gradually developed, being handed down through the generations. These are now known as traditional English quilting designs and many can be seen in local and national museums. Each one has a different story to tell, particular signs and stitches being used in different localities.

Fabrics
Many fabrics are suitable for quilting, but the easiest to use are those made from natural fibres. Choose smooth, closely woven fabrics such as dress or lightweight furnishing cottons, fine linen or silk. Man-made fibres are more difficult to handle than natural ones, as they are very springy and do not quilt easily. Light colours show up more effectively than dark ones. Make sure the fabric is pressed carefully before use, as creases cannot be removed when the quilting has been worked.

Padding
For the padding use synthetic wadding, which comes in many thicknesses. This is light, easy to use and washes well. Only a thin layer is necessary as a rule. Alternatively, for less padded quilting use domette or bump, but neither of these is washable.

Backing
When the backing will be visible, use the same fabric as for the top layer, as with a cot quilt or bed covers. When the backing will be hidden (i.e. on cushions, teapot covers, bedheads, photograph frames, etc.) use calico, butter muslin, organdie or mull.

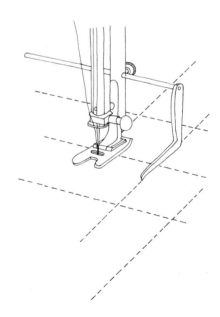

Fig. 139 *Using a quilting gauge to keep equal distances between the stitching*

Threads

Match the threads to the fabrics where possible, i.e. cotton on cotton, silk on silk. Use Sylko, buttonhole twist, pure silk, stranded embroidery cottons, cotton perle. Match the colour to the fabric, and if necessary have a darker, not a lighter tone. Do not use contrasting coloured threads, for these are not really attractive.

Stitches

By hand: Use running stitch, back stitch or chain stitch.
By machine: Use straight stitch or zigzag stitch, or a combination of both. Use a quilting gauge for straight lines to maintain equal distances between the lines of stitching (*fig. 139*). Use a strong needle with a loose tension and medium size stitch.

Designs

The object of wadded quilting is to hold the three pieces of fabric together, so when des-

Fig. 140 *Some traditional quilting designs*

Fig. 141 *Transferring the design using tissue paper and small running stitches*

igning for quilting remember that to be successful the stitching must be evenly worked over the whole area. Make original templates or patterns using natural or geometric shapes (e.g. leaves, flowers, diamonds, ovals and circles). Select a group of templates and arrange them so that they fit into the area to be quilted. Do not fill the whole space with the patterns, but leave some of the area free for the background filling stitches. This shows up the design to advantage. Some traditional quilting designs (*fig. 140*) can be obtained in transfer form from craft and needlework shops.

Quilting can also be worked on printed fabrics, outlining the design on the material, provided it is not too complicated. Pick out suitable motifs for quilting and aim for a balanced effect, always making sure that the stitching is evenly distributed. This can be worked by hand or machine.

Transferring the design

The design must be marked on to the right side of the top layer of fabric and this is best done in the following way. Trace the design onto tissue paper and tack it onto the fabric round the four sides. Work a running stitch round the outline of the design in a contrasting coloured thread, through both paper and fabric (*fig. 141*). Unpick the tacking stitches at the four edges and carefully tear away the tissue paper. This leaves the design outlined and ready for quilting. Remove these stitches as the quilting is worked. Alternatively, the design can be marked by scratching it on to the fabric using a large blunt needle, being careful not to damage the fabric (*fig. 142*). Not all fabrics mark satisfactorily when this method is used, particularly those with a high percentage of man-made fibres.

The design can also be traced on to the fabric using dressmaker's carbon paper. This is not as satisfactory as the two previous methods described, as it is sometimes difficult to remove the markings. However, it will wash out. Trace the design on to tracing paper and pin it in position on the right side of the fabric. Slip the carbon paper under the tracing, carbon side down, and use a sharp pencil to outline the design, which will then be transferred to the fabric.

Finishing

The edges of quilting can be finished in three ways, depending on the article being made.

(i) Turn in the top layer of fabric and the backing fabric 1.3 cm (½ in) and work a line of running stitches as close as possible to the edge. Work a second row of stitching 6 mm (¼ in) from the first (*fig. 143*).

(ii) Pipe the edge using crossway strip 2.5—3.8 cm (1—1½ in) wide and a fine piping cord. Turn in the raw edges of the top layer of fabric and the backing fabric 1.3 cm (½ in). Tack the piping cord into the crossway strip and insert it between the two layers of fabric. Pin and tack into position. Stitch by hand using running stitches to match the rest of the work. (*fig. 144*).

(iii) Bind the raw edges of the quilting with crossway strip 3.8 cm (1½ in) wide cut from matching fabric.

Instructions are given for making a baby's carry cot cover. This gives the basic techniques for quilting and can be adapted when larger quilts or other items are being made, e.g. cushion covers, bed head covers, bedspreads, tea pot covers and so on.

Fig. 142 *Marking round the design with a blunt needle*

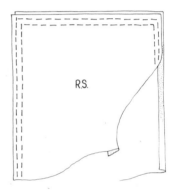

Fig. 143 *Finishing the edges of quilting with two rows of running stitches*

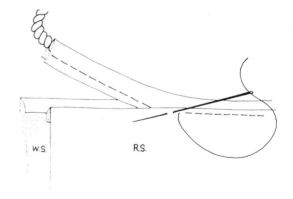

Fig. 144 *Inserting piping cord and crossway strip between two layers of fabric to finish the edges of quilting*

Quilted cot cover (or a carry cot or moses basket)

2 pieces of fabric approx. 61 x 51 cm (24 x 20 in) for the top and bottom layers. Choose washable fabrics, either plain or with a small repeating design (use ginghams, lawns or light dress cottons).

Synthetic wadding 58.5 x 48.5 cm (23 x 19 in).

Card for making templates.

Paper for drafting out the design.

(1) Cut out the quilt fabric for the top and bottom layers to the size required plus 2.5 cm (1 in) for turnings (this allows for some fabric being taken up in the quilting process). Press. Cut out the wadding to the same size.

(2) Cut out templates of traditional quilting designs, or draw round cups, plates, flowers or leaves to make suitable patterns. Templates can also be made by folding a strip of paper and cutting out simple shapes (*fig. 146*). These can then be stuck onto a piece of card and cut out. Plan the design onto a piece of paper the size of the finished quilt.

Fig. 145 *Design for a cot quilt showing tacking lines*

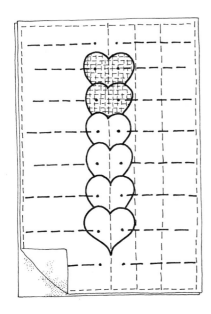

Fig. 146 *Making a simple template from folded paper*

(3) Transfer or mark the design onto the right side of the top layer of fabric (see the earlier section in this chapter).

(4) Sandwich the wadding between the top and bottom layers of fabric with the right sides outside. To prevent the layers of fabric moving whilst it is being quilted tack them together firmly. If a large piece of work is being quilted it is also best to use a large embroidery frame to hold it securely in position and to prevent a puckered effect when finished. However, small pieces can be quilted satisfactorily in the hand, provided they are tacked up carefully.

(5) Smooth the fabric out, and starting from the centre of the work make a row of tacking stitches out to the edge of the fabric every 3.8–5 cm (1½–2 in) across the work (*fig. 145*). Tack round the outer edge.

(6) Stitch round the design, using running stitch, back stitch or chain stitch, or a combination of all three. Keep the stitching even and regular and work outwards from the centre through the three layers of fabric.

(7) When the main designs have been quilted, fill in the background with horizontal or diagonal lines 2.5–3.8 cm (1–1½ in) apart, marking out guide lines on the fabric with a ruler and tacking stitches or tailor's chalk.

(8) When all the quilting has been worked, take out the tacking stitches and finish the edges using one of the methods given earlier. Alternatively, a gathered or pleated frill can be applied (see Chapter 4).

Lining a Baby's Basket or Crib

The techniques used for lining this basket can be adapted and applied when lining carry cots or moses baskets, or when lining sewing baskets, make-up baskets or picnic baskets (*fig. 147*).

Baby basket
Quilted fabric for the lining (ready quilted or hand quilted).
Card or heavyweight interfacing (Vilene) for the base.
Brown paper for making the pattern.

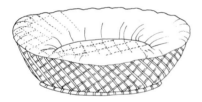

Fig. 147 *Lining a basket using quilted fabric*

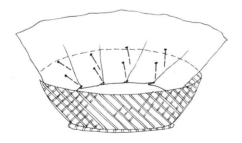

Fig. 148 *Making a pattern of the basket by pinning tucks in the paper to get a good fit*

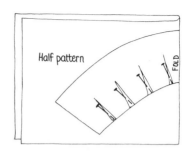

Fig. 149 *Making the pattern for the side section*

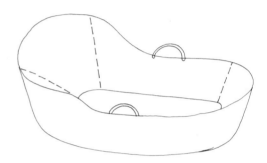

Fig. 150 *Pattern sections marked for a moses basket*

(1) Make a paper pattern of the inside of the basket in order to estimate the amount of fabric required by placing a piece of brown paper or newspaper on the bottom of the basket and pressing down firmly to get an indented line round the base. Cut round this mark. With a pencil or a coloured thread mark one half of the basket. Fit a strip of paper to the inside of the basket on the one half only. Press down at the base and make tucks in the sides where necessary to make the paper fit (*fig. 148*). Mark round the paper at the top of the basket with a felt tip pen and cut along this line. Place this half pattern to the fold on a larger piece of paper and cut out (*fig. 149*). Open out the pattern and try it inside the basket. Adjust to fit, trimming away surplus paper where necessary.

(2) When lining a moses basket or a crib it is best to make the pattern in sections, one for each side and one for the head and foot of the crib (*fig. 150*). When making the base pattern, tuck the paper firmly into the corners and along the edges to get as accurate a pattern as possible. Cut out as before.

(3) To make the lining cut out the quilted fabric for the base and side sections using the paper patterns. Add 1.3 cm (½ in) seam allowance all round except at the top edge of the side section. Here, 3.8 cm (1½ in) must be added to allow for seams and for neatening of the top edge (see 7 below). When making a lining for a moses basket or a crib remember to reverse the two side pieces so as to have one left and one right side. Allow 2.5 cm (1 in) turnings.

(4) Join the side sections with 1.3 (½ in) turnings to make a circular piece. Press seam open. Place this in the basket with the wrong side facing outwards. If necessary, adjust the fabric with darts to make it fit well.

(5) Make a line of gathering stitches round the outer edge of the base section. Place the base section to the circular side section with right sides together, and pin and tack into position. Take

Fig. 151 *Lacing the fabric on the wrong side*

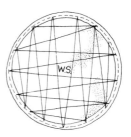

Fig. 152 *Velcro sewn to the basket and the lining to make it detachable*

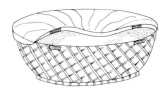

Fig. 153 *Gathered and pleated frills used on babies' cribs*

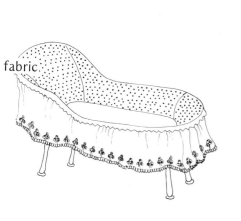

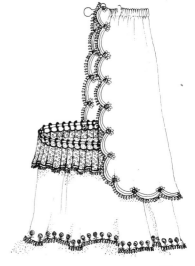

1.3 cm (½ in) turnings and ease where necessary. Machine stitch. Drop into the basket to check that it fits well.

(6) Cut out a shape in cardboard 6 mm (¼ in) smaller than the base section, using the paper pattern as a guide. Place the card on the wrong side of the base section and pull up the gathering thread so that it is held in position. With a long thread lace the fabric across the wrong side as in fig. 151 to hold it firmly in place. Omit this process when a fully washable detachable lining is required, or instead use a piece of heavyweight interfacing (Vilene) or other washable interfacing.

(7) At the top of the side section turn down the raw edge 1.3 cm (½ in) and fold over to the top outer edge of the basket. Stab stitch through the fabric and the basket, keeping the stitches as inconspicuous as possible, to hold the lining permanently in position. To make the lining detachable, make a 1.3 cm (½ in) double hem at the top edge of the side section and machine into place. Fix the basket with three or four pieces of Velcro touch-and-close fastening. Sew this on by hand to both the basket and the lining (fig. 152).

(8) A gathered or pleated frill can be made and sewn to the top edge of the basket or crib following the instructions in Chapter 4 (fig. 153).

(9) For a basket with handles, slash the fabric to fit round the handles and neaten the raw edges with bias binding or crossway strip made in matching fabric

Hanging Holdalls

These can be made with or without a waterproof lining and can be used to take toys, laundry, shoes or any odds and ends (fig. 154). A smaller version of this holdall makes a useful peg bag.

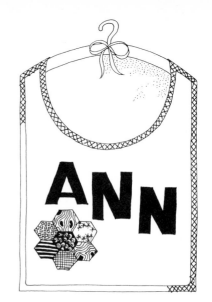

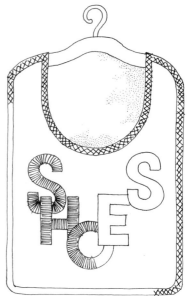

Fig. 154 *Hanging holdalls*

2 pieces of fabric 45.5 cm (18 in) x 58.5 cm (23 in). Choose strong furnishing cotton, sailcloth or canvas.
2 pieces of waterproof fabric. Choose nylon or plastic shower curtain fabric (optional).
29 cm (9 in) contrasting fabric for binding.
1 wooden coat hanger.
Scraps of felt or fabric for appliqué motifs.
Stencil for letters.
Patchwork motif (optional).

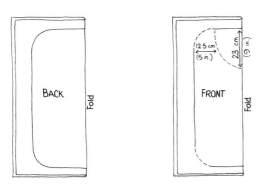

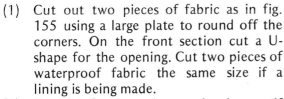

Fig. 155 *Cutting out fabric for a hanging holdall*

Fig. 156 *Waterproof lining tacked to the front section*

(1) Cut out two pieces of fabric as in fig. 155 using a large plate to round off the corners. On the front section cut a U-shape for the opening. Cut two pieces of waterproof fabric the same size if a lining is being made.

(2) On the front section apply the motif of patchwork (see Chapter 9). Using stencils, cut out felt initials and apply them with a herringbone stitch or a good adhesive. (When drawing out the letters place the stencil in reverse on the back of the felt.)

(3) Place the waterproof lining on the wrong side of the front section and tack in position all round (*fig. 156*).

(4) Prepare and cut out crossway strip 3.8 cm (1½ in) wide from the contrasting fabric, using the quick method described in Chapter 4. Bind the opening on the front section with bias strip. Trim seams and clip the curves (*fig. 156*).

(5) Line the back section of the holdall in the same way as the front section (see (3) above).

(6) Place the wrong side of the front section to the wrong side of the back section and pin and tack into position (*fig. 157*). Machine stitch and trim seams to 6 mm (¼ in) and clip curves.

(7) Apply the crossway strip to the four sides, joining the ends as in Chapter 4.

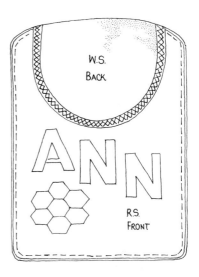

Fig. 157 *The front and back sections tacked into position*

Slip the wooden hanger into the opening of the holdall. This can be padded and covered to match the holdall following the instructions in Chapter 11.

Christmas Stockings

Christmas stockings can be made for all the family. These are simple and fun to make and should last for many years. They make

Fig. 158 *Ideas for motifs for Christmas stockings*

Fig. 159 *Christmas stockings for all the family*

useful presents for young children and are amusing for the older members of the family, particularly when decorated to suit individual needs. Smaller versions of these stockings can be made to hang on the Christmas tree, filled with tiny gifts or goodies.

45.5 cm (18 in) square of felt makes one
    stocking approx. 43 x 18 cm (17 x 7 in).
Oddments of felt for appliqué shapes.
Sequins, beads, cords, braids, ribbons for
    trimming.
Stencils for letters of names and initials.
Lurex embroidery yarn.

(1) Cut out a paper pattern of a stocking shape using a sock as a guide (*fig. 159*). From this pattern cut two pieces of felt.

(2) Decorate one or both sides of the stocking using small pieces of coloured felt to make motifs of trees, snowmen, soldiers, etc. (*fig. 160*). Use stencils to cut out letters for names and initials. Remember to reverse the stencils and draw round them on the back of the felt. Appliqué the motifs by sewing with herringbone stitch (*fig. 14*) or apply them with a good adhesive. Sew on narrow cords and braids with couching stitch (*fig. 161*) and make sure sequins and buttons are sewn on securely.

(3) When the front and back sections have been decorated, pin and tack the two sections together with wrong sides facing. Stitch round the three sides of the stocking with embroidery thread using blanket stitch (*fig. 7*). A thick lurex embroidery yarn gives an attractive result. Alternatively, machine stitch first for extra strength.

(4) Cut a piece of felt 30.5 cm (12 in) long x 3.8 cm (1½ in) wide for the loop at the top of the stocking. Fold in half lengthwise and machine down one long side. Pin in position at the top of the stocking and sew in place firmly.

(5) For the turnover at the top of the stocking cut a piece of white felt long enough to fit round the top edge and 5—6.4 cm (2—2½ in) wide. Cut one long side in a zigzag shape and apply round the top edge of the stocking having the join at the back. Alternatively, apply a straight piece of white synthetic fur fabric to the top edge of the stocking.

Fig. 160 *Cutting out a stocking shape*

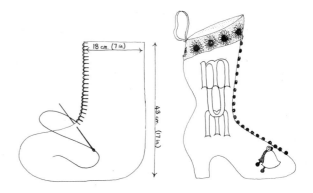

Fig. 161 *Couching stitch used for sewing on narrow cords and braids*

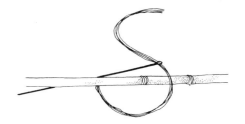

9

THE DINING ROOM

Attractive inexpensive table linen can be made from easy care fabrics that need little or no ironing. Make tablecloths and place mats for all seasons from printed or plain polyester/cotton sheeting, felt, or evenly woven fabrics which do not stretch or fray. Choose washable plain or co-ordinating fabrics or ones with an all-over design with small motifs or patterns. Ginghams, checks and spots work well for table linen, as do seersucker, 'linen look' acrylic fabrics and polyester/cotton sheeting. Remnants can be used effectively to make table napkins and place mats and can be made to match or complement the table china.

Experiment with colours and fabrics to make different table settings for special occasions. These can be relatively inexpensive and most rewarding, and can be matched to wallpaper, curtains or blinds. Tablecloths for Christmas and for children's birthday parties can be made, and with a little imagination and skill most attractive and original results achieved.

Small round tables can be covered with circular cloths draped to the floor, providing very attractive bedside or display tables. Smaller circular or square cloths in co-ordinating fabric can be made for covering the top, which is also a practical way of treating a dining room table.

Fitted tablecloths can be made for kitchen and dining room tables, but when making these, first ensure that the fabric is shrink resistant.

To protect polished surfaces from hot plates buy special heat-resistant material to put underneath the tablecloth. This is made from a mixture of latex rubber and cotton and can be cut to the exact size of the table top. It is available in a range of colours and widths.

The amount of fabric needed for tablecloths depends on the size and shape of the table and the width of the fabric. Always buy the widest fabric possible in order to avoid the necessity for seams. With a floor length cloth, however, these are usually inevitable, but you can make the seams at the sides, matching patterns carefully so that the seams are as inconspicuous as possible (*fig. 163*).

Tablecloths

Square and rectangular tablecloths
Estimate the amount of fabric required by measuring the top of the table and allowing for a generous overhang on all sides (approximately 25.5–30.5 cm (10–12 in). To this measurement add 2.5 cm (1 in) all round for making a plain hem. Alternatively, the raw edges can be bound with crossway strip made from matching or co-ordinating fabrics, or trimmed with fringe or other decorative edging.

If it is necessary to join widths of fabric together, position the seams so that they are as unobtrusive as possible, usually with a wide panel in the centre of the table (*fig. 163*). Match any patterns carefully. Use flat fell or French seams (see Chapter 4) or use a plain seam on the right side. Trim this down to

6 mm (¼ in) and cover the raw edges with braid, ribbon or a co-ordinating or contrasting piece of fabric.

(1) Cut out the fabric widths and cut off all selvedges. Join widths together with seams as explained above and round off corners; if necessary using a large plate as a guide.

(2) To make a plain hem, fold over the raw edges 6 mm (¼ in) to the wrong side of the cloth and press. Then fold over 2.5 cm (1 in) and press. Open out the last fold and mitre the corners as in figs. 22–26, cutting away the corner to 6 mm (¼ in) (*fig. 164*). Re-fold the hem and tack into position. Machine stitch 6 mm (¼ in) from the folded edges as in fig. 165 and slip stitch by hand. Alternatively, use a decorative embroidery stitch to hold the hem in position.

(3) On plain tablecloths motifs can be appliquéd to the cloth using herringbone stitch or machine zigzag. Or small pieces of Velcro can be applied to both motif and cloth, which makes them interchangeable so that the tablecloth can be used for many different occasions.

Fig. 162 *Ideas for tablecloths*

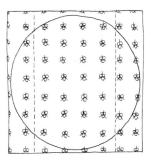

Fig. 163 *Joining fabric widths together*

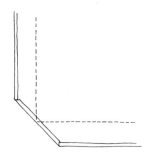

Fig. 164 *Mitring the corner on a tablecloth*

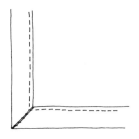

Fig. 165 *Finishing the hem of a tablecloth*

Fitted floor length tablecloth

(1) For a rectangular or square tablecloth, cut out the fabric to the size of the table top allowing 1.3 cm (½ in) turnings all round. For the skirt cut four separate sections, each measuring the length of each side of the table plus 20.5 cm (8 in) (for each corner pleat) by the height of the table, plus 5 cm (2 in) (for turnings and hem) (*fig. 166*).

(2) Join the four side sections together with French seams. At the lower edge turn up a 1.3 cm (½ in) double hem. Tack and machine into position.

(3) With the right sides together pin and tack the side sections to the top section, taking 1.3 cm (½ in) turnings. Make a 10 cm (4 in) inverted pleat at each corner of the cloth, positioning the seams in the pleats so that they are as unobtrusive as possible.

Circular tablecloth

This can be made in different lengths to fit any round table. The edges can be scalloped, machine embroidered or bound with cross-way strip.

(1) To estimate the amount of fabric needed find the centre of the table and with a tape measure take the measurement from this point down to the floor, or to the length required (this is the radius) (*fig. 167*). Double this measurement to obtain the diameter of the tablecloth. If the figure obtained is greater than the measurement of the width of the fabric it will be necessary to join the fabric widths together (*fig. 163*) before the circle of material is cut out.

(2) To cut a circle, make a paper pattern first to the size required. To do this take a square piece of newspaper large enough to make the circle. Fold it into four so that each side of the square measures a little more than the radius of the tablecloth (*fig. 168*).

(3) Tie one end of a piece of string to a pencil as near to its point as possible. Take the radius measurement of the tablecloth and mark this on the string with a drawing pin. Secure the pin at this point into one corner of the folded paper. Holding the pencil upright, draw an arc from A to B, keeping the string taut (*fig. 168*). Cut out along the pencil line through all thicknesses of the paper, to obtain the circle.

Fig. 166 *Cutting out sections for a fitted tablecloth*

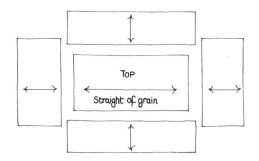

(4) Fold the fabric for the tablecloth lengthwise and cut out the fabric using one
half of the paper pattern only (*fig. 169*).
If a large cloth is being made fold the
fabric lengthwise and widthwise first
before using only one quarter of the pattern to cut out the fabric.

(5) Finish the edges of the tablecloth with
a machine embroidery stitch, scallops,
frill or binding (Chapter 4).

(6) Motifs of flowers, patchwork or other
simple shapes could be applied to the
cloth with a machine zigzag stitch. Cut
out the shapes first in iron-on interfacing (Vilene). Iron these on to the
back of the fabric before cutting out the
motifs. Pin and tack the motifs to the
cloth and machine zigzag round each
one (*fig. 162*).

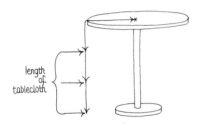

Fig. 167 *Taking measurements for a circular
tablecloth. Finding the radius*

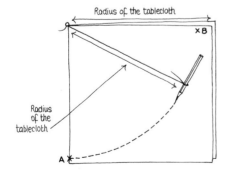

Fig. 168 *Making a pattern for a circular
tablecloth*

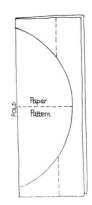

Fig. 169 *Cutting out the fabric using the
paper pattern*

Table Napkins

Table napkins can match place mats or tablecloths and are very simple to make. One
metre of 91.5 cm (36 in) wide fabric makes
four napkins 45.5 cm (18 in) square. Use
easy-care washable fabrics, as for tablecloths,
and make them in matching, contrasting or
co-ordinating fabrics to team up with tablecloths or place mats.

Finish the raw edges by turning in 6 mm
(¼ in) double hem. Press well and stitch by
machine using a straight or zigzag stitch. A
hemstitching needle gives a professional
result on suitable fabrics. Alternatively, make
scalloped edges with an automatic machine
embroidery stitch. This looks more effective
on smaller items of table linen such as place
mats or napkins (*fig. 170*). The edges could
also be bound with bias binding or trimmed
with lace, but first make sure that these will
withstand regular laundering.

Even-weave fabrics can be machine stitched
2.5 cm (1 in) in from the edge all round and
then frayed by removing the threads up to
the stitching (*fig. 171*).

Place Mats

Place mats can be made in simple shapes such
as hearts and flowers as well as in the usual
rectangular, square or circular shapes. (*fig.
172*).

91

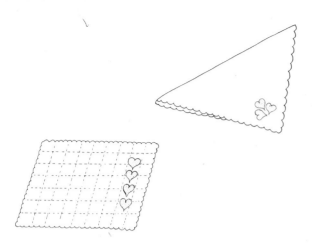

Fig. 170 *Machine scallops used to finish the edge of a table napkin*

Fig. 173 *Placemats made in patchwork*

Fig. 171 *Fraying the edges on evenweave fabric*

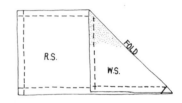

Fig. 174 *Working the corner of a rectangular mat*

Fig. 172 *Heart-shaped mats bound with crossway strip in co-ordinating fabric*

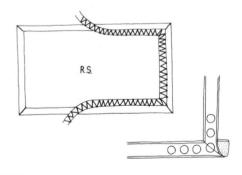

Fig. 175 *Folding braid over the mitred corners*

Decide on the best size for the mat by laying one place setting and measuring the area used. An average size for a circular mat is approximately 25.5 cm (10 in) and for a rectangular shape approximately 38 x 30.5 cm (15 x 12 in), but these sizes can be varied to suit individual requirements.

Use washable fabrics in evenweave 'linen look' acrylics, poplins or cottons, or use ready quilted fabrics, or quilt your own to match other soft furnishings. Alternatively, use large patchwork motifs to make attractive mats, or make smaller motifs and appliqué them to plain mats.

6 *Curtains and pleated valance match the squab cushion on the chair*

Special heat-resistant material made from latex rubber and cotton, mentioned earlier, can be sandwiched between two layers of fabric to make the mat heat resistant.

Finish the edges of the mats with machine embroidery, or bind them with crossway strip made in matching or contrasting fabric. Alternatively, on reversible fabric turn up a 2.5 cm (1 in) hem to the right side of the fabric and press well. Fold over one corner diagonally as in fig. 174 and make a seam at right angles to the fold. Trim seam to 6 mm (¼ in). Turn the corner to the right side and press well. Mitre each corner in the same way and turn right sides out. Stitch braid over the raw edges on the right side of the mat, folding the braid over the mitred corners as in fig. 175.

Patchwork

Patchwork is a practical way of using up odd pieces of fabric left over from other home sewing projects. Small or large patches of various shapes can be cut and sewn together to make cushions and bedspreads, or used to decorate such things as curtains, table mats and pillow cases. With a knowledge of the basic skills, interesting and original designs can be made using the patchwork templates that are readily obtainable. Rigid templates should be used to cut out the paper shape required for each patch.

A piece of fabric is then cut from the shape allowing appropriate turnings and is tacked to the paper shape. The patches are sewn together and the paper removed when the work is finished. The following notes on the basic principles of patchwork may serve as a useful guide for the beginner wishing to start this craft. There are many specialist books on the subject for those wishing to proceed further (see Bibliography).

Templates. These should be made from metal, Perpex or Plexiglass and are available in various shapes and sizes. The shapes are mostly geometric, the hexagon being the one most often used by the beginner. However, the same principles apply to all geometric shapes.

Fabrics. Choose fabrics that are of a similar weight and texture and which fold well. Avoid those that stretch or fray easily as these are difficult to handle. If an article needs regular laundering (e.g. place mats or pillow cases) make sure that all the fabrics used are easily washable and colour fast.

Card. Use stiff paper or thin card for cutting out the shapes from the templates and use an old pair of scissors for cutting.

Threads. Use pure silk if using silk fabrics, synthetic thread for man-made fibres and cotton (No. 40—100) for cotton fabrics. Use black thread for sewing dark patches together and white for sewing light patches together.

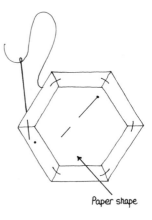

Fig. 176 *Tacking the fabric to the paper shape*

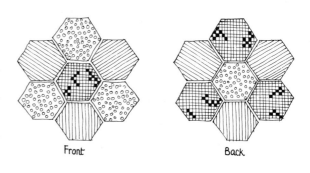

Front   Back

Fig. 177 *Planning the design for the table mat using hexagons*

Instructions are given below for making a table mat from a hexagon shape template. This gives the basic techniques for patchwork and these can be adapted and used when other items are being made.

Patchwork place mat
7.5 cm (3 in) hexagon template.
4 small pieces of different fabrics for the patches.
Synthetic wadding.
Stiff paper or card.

(1) Draw round the template very carefully on the stiff paper or card using a sharp pencil. Cut out on the pencil line. Cut out 14 shapes in this way (seven for the front of the mat and seven for the back). Cut them out as accurately as possible so that they match up well.

(2) Pin the paper shape to the wrong side of the selected fabric and cut out, adding a seam allowance of 1 cm ($\frac{3}{8}$ in) all round. Centre the pattern if necessary, using a window template. This is a template with a hole in the middle the size of the finished patch, the outer edge representing the seam allowance. The template is laid onto the fabric and patterns can be positioned for each patch.

(3) Fold the seam allowance over the edge of the paper, keeping the template parallel to the grain of the fabric. Tack as in fig. 176. If using fabrics that are marked easily by the needle, do not tack right through to the right side of the fabric but take the tacking stitches into the paper only.

(4) Plan the design for the seven-shaped motif for the front and back sections of the table mat and lay them in position (*fig. 177*). Take the centre patch from one motif and from one of the outer patches and place them with the right sides together. Oversew them with a single thread and small, even stitches, using a fine needle. Insert the needle at right angles and start as near as possible

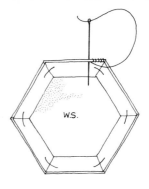

Fig. 178   *Sewing the patches together*

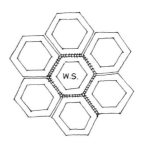

Fig. 179   *Method of stitching*

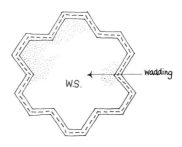

Fig. 180   *The wadding tacked into position*

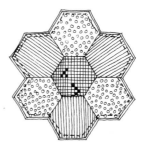

Fig. 181   *Stitching round the outer edge*

to one corner, working in the end of the thread as shown in fig. 178. Work all round the centre patch oversewing each of the six patches to it (*fig. 179*), then complete the motif by sewing the centre patch out to the edge of each of the outer patches. Fasten off by working backwards for two or three stitches. The stitches are not meant to be invisible on the right side of the work, but they should be worked as evenly as possible to give a neat appearance.

(5) Press the two pieces gently with a warm iron on the wrong side of the motifs. Unpick the tacking stitches and remove all the paper.

(6) Cut out a piece of thin synthetic wadding or interlining to the size of the mat and apply this to one of the two motifs, tacking it in position under the seam allowance at the outer edge (*fig. 180*).

(7) With the wrong sides facing, place the two motifs together and slip stitch round all sides. Alternatively, machine stitch or hand stitch round the outer edge as in fig. 181.

Bread Roll Holder

This is a useful holder for rolls, biscuits, eggs or fruit, but can also be made into a dressing table tidy to hold make up, manicure requisites, etc. Use washable fabrics that look alike on both sides. Ginghams, poplins, and broderie anglaise work well and can be lightly starched when washed for crisp results.

Fig. 182 *Bread roll holder*

Fig. 183 *Tacking and machining the trimming into position using a zigzag stitch*

Fig. 184 *Folding the circles into six sections*

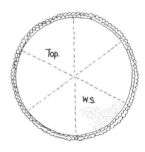

Fig. 185 *Marking the top and middle circles into six equal sections*

30.5 cm (18 in) 91.5 cm (36 in) wide fabric. (Choose poly/cotton gaberdine, gingham, broderie anglaise.)

3 m (3¼ yd) guipure lace trimming, bias binding or crossway strip in contrasting fabric.

2 snap fasteners.

96

3 Table mats, tablecloth and table napkins made to complement the cushions and chair covers

4 Co-ordinated fabrics used effectively for loose covers, bedspread, dressing table and pillows

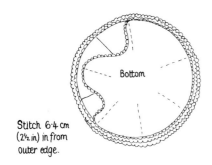

Stitch 6·4 cm
(2½ in) in from
outer edge.

Fig. 186 *Machining the bottom circle to the top and middle sections*

Fig. 187 *Positions for snap fasteners on the top section*

(1) Cut out three circles of fabric 28 cm (11 in) in diameter, using a large plate or tray as a guide.

(2) Pin and tack the lace edging over the raw edges of each circle of fabric. Machine stitch in position using a small, close zigzag stitch (*fig. 183*).

(3) If using crossway strip to neaten the raw edges cut this using the method described in Chapter 4 and apply it to each circle, joining it as in Chapter 4.

(4) Place the top and middle circles together with right sides facing. Divide into six equal sections by folding first in half and then in three (*fig. 184*). Mark the sections with pins and then a tacking line, and machine stitch along this line. Do not stitch over the edging (*fig. 185*).

(5) Apply the bottom circle to the other two circles and pin and tack between the sections of the top two circles as in fig. 186. Machine stitch from the outer edge of the circle for 6.4 cm (2½ in), or sew by hand using a back stitch.

(6) Turn the circles over to the right side and sew on snap fasteners in the positions shown in fig. 187.

(7) Use the holder in a small basket.

10

THE KITCHEN

Many attractive and useful items can be made for the kitchen turning it into a comfortable place for all members of the family to work, eat and play in.

In addition to the curtains, roller blinds, tablecloths and napkins described in previous chapters, further accessories can complete the decorative scheme.

Squab Cushions

These are both decorative and functional, for they provide comfortable seating on kitchen benches and chairs and can be made to match curtains, blinds or other kitchen accessories. Choose firm, washable fabrics that do not stretch easily. Printed furnishing cottons and

good quality ginghams can be both effective and hard wearing and are an ideal choice for the kitchen of today.

Plastic or latex foam 2.5 cm (1 in) thick.
No. 3 piping cord.
50 cm (18 in) 122 cm (48 in) wide fabric
    makes two average size squab cushions.
Toggles (optional).

(1) Make a paper pattern of the chair seat. Lay a piece of newspaper or brown paper on the seat and draw round the front, sides and back so that the pattern fits well. Before cutting out, fold the pattern in half lengthwise to make sure that each side is cut the same (*fig. 189*). Try the pattern on the chair to check fit, and adjust or trim as necessary.

Fig. 188 *Ideas for the kitchen using simple techniques*

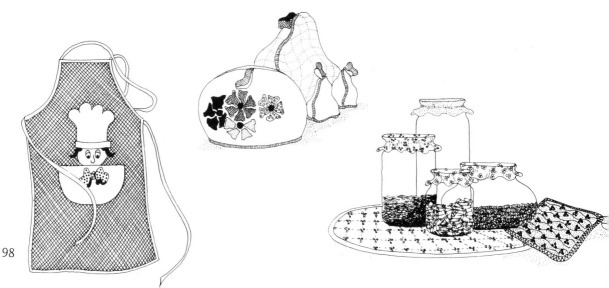

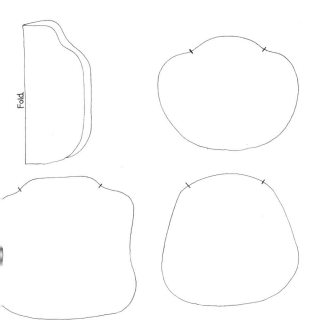

Fig. 189 *Some shapes for squab cushions showing positions for openings at the back of the cushions*

(2) Lay the pattern on a piece of plastic foam and draw round it with a felt tip pen. For a cushion without a welt use foam approximately 2.5 cm (1 in) thick, cutting it with a sharp pair of scissors. Thicker foam can be cut with a sharp knife. Make a cover for the foam in calico or cotton to protect it (Chapter 7).

(3) Cut out two pieces of fabric to the size of the paper pattern plus 2.5 cm (1 in) all round. This allows for the thickness of the foam and for 1.3 cm (½ in) turnings. Centralize any patterns or motifs.

(4) Prepare enough crossway strip to fit round the sides of the cushion plus a little extra. Use the quick method of cutting described in Chapter 4. Tack the crossway strip and the piping cord to the right side of the front section of the cover, tacking close to the cord, and clipping curves where necessary (*fig. 58*). Machine into position.

(5) To make ties to hold the cushion to the chair cut strips of fabric 3.2 cm (1¼ in) wide on the straight grain, long enough to make two ties — about 61 cm (24 in). Fold in half lengthwise and press. Machine all round. Mark the positions for the ties and apply the front section of the cover, stitching firmly into position as in fig. 190.

(6) Alternatively, the cushion can be attached to the chair with a decorative toggle fastening and loops. Make the loops by cutting four pieces of fabric approximately 20.5 x 5 cm (8 x 2 in). Fold in the long edges to the wrong side 1.3 cm (½ in) wide and press. Fold again to make a strip 1.3 cm (½ in) wide and machine the two folded edges together. Fold two of the four strips as in fig. 191 leaving a loop in which to insert and sew the toggle. Slip stitch the two edges firmly together as in fig. 191. Fold and stitch the two other strips in the same way but leaving a loop large enough to use with the toggle. Mark the positions on the cushion cover for the loops and toggles so that they fit round the back of the chair (*fig. 192*). Apply in pairs to the front section of the cover, stitching firmly in position over the piping cord and crossway strip (*fig. 190*). Insert the toggles and sew in position when the cushion cover is complete.

Fig. 190 *Stitching ties to the front section of the cushion*

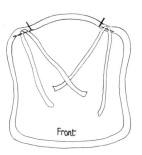

Fig. 191 *Making a loop for a toggle fastening*

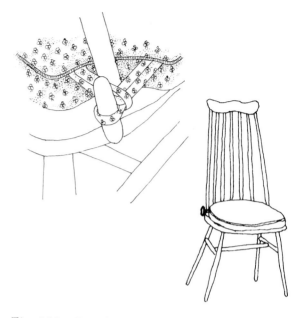

(7) Pin and tack the top section to the bottom section of the cushion cover, leaving an opening across the back edge. Machine, clip curves and neaten raw edges. Insert the foam pad and slip stitch the opening together. Alternatively, bind the opening and apply touch-and-close fastening (Velcro).

Fig. 192 *Toggle fastening at the back of the chair*

Hostess Apron

Aprons can be made quickly and easily from fabric remnants or can be made to match or co-ordinate with other accessories. Instructions are given below for a hostess apron which protects a long skirt or dress. A short version of this could be made by omitting the frill. Choose cotton or polyester/cotton fabrics that wash well. Polyester/cotton sheeting cuts to advantage.

1 m (1¼ yd) 91.5 cm (36 in) wide printed cotton fabric.

1 m (1 yd) 91.5 cm (36 in) wide co-ordinating or plain cotton fabric.

(1) Cut out the apron using the cutting plan in fig. 194.
(2) Turn over a 6 mm (¼ in) double hem at the top edge of the bodice. Tack and machine into position.
(3) Turn over a 6 mm (¼ in) hem at each side of the straps and press. Apply the straps to each side of the bodice as in fig. 195, tacking and machining into position.

Fig. 193 *Hostess apron using plain and patterned fabrics*

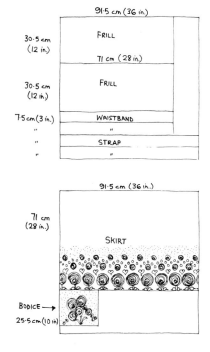

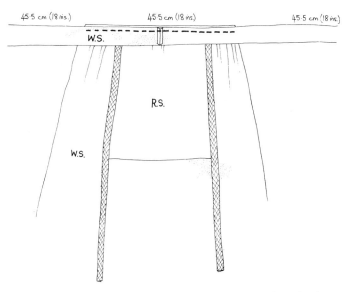

Fig. 196   *The bodice and waistband tacked into position*

Fig. 194   *Cutting plan for a hostess apron*

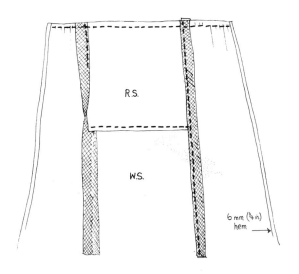

Fig. 195   *The straps applied to the bodice section*

(4)   Turn over a 6 mm (¼ in) double hem at each side of the skirt. Tack and machine into position. Work two rows of gathering stitches along the top edge of the skirt and draw up to measure 45.5 cm (18 in).

(5)   With right sides together join the two waistband sections along the short sides with a 1.3 cm (½ in) flat seam, and press open. Trim seam to 6 mm (¼ in).

(6)   With wrong sides together pin and tack the bodice to the centre of the gathered edge of the skirt (*fig. 196*). With right sides facing, pin and tack the waistband to the bodice at the top edge, positioning it so that it is in the middle of the skirt section (*fig. 196*). Machine the waistband and the bodice in position.

(7)   Turn in the waistband along the long edges 1.3 cm (½ in) and fold over on to the right side of the skirt. Tack and machine all along the lower edge of the waistband, neatening each end by turning in 6 mm (¼ in). Tack and machine the upper edge of the waistband to the bodice.

(8) Join the two frill pieces along the short sides with a French seam. Tack and machine a 6 mm (¼ in) double hem along the two sides and along the lower edge of the frill. Make two rows of gathering stitches along the upper edge of the frill and pull up to fit the lower edge of the skirt. With wrong sides facing, attach the frill to the skirt adjusting the gathers evenly. Work a French seam (see Chapter 4) to complete the apron.

P.V.C. Apron

Aprons made from polyvinyl chloride are very versatile and hard-wearing and can easily be sponged clean or washed by hand in warm water. The fabric is very sensitive to heat and cannot be ironed.

When working with p.v.c. do not pin or tack the fabric as this would damage it. Hold seams in place if necessary with sticky tape or paper clips. Machine rather than hand sew, using a long stitch and a needle suitable for medium to heavy weight fabrics. If the fabric is very shiny and does not slide properly beneath the presser foot use tissue paper underneath the fabric to prevent it from sticking. Alternatively, spread a little talcum powder on the shiny side of the fabric to lubricate it through the machine or use a special presser foot with sliding rolls.

75 cm (27 in) p.v.c. printed fabric 114.5 cm (45 in) wide.

1.75 m (1¾ yd) strong cotton tape 2.5 cm (1 in) wide.

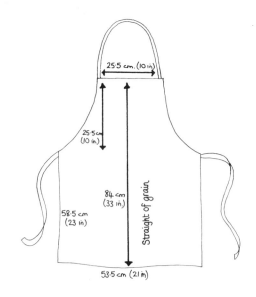

Fig. 197 *Guide for cutting a p.v.c. apron*

(1) Cut out a paper pattern using fig. 197 as a guide.

(2) Fold the fabric in half lengthwise and cut out the fabric using one half of the pattern only, marking the fabric on the wrong side with a soft pencil.

(3) Cut two pieces of tape 45.5 cm (18 in) long for the ties at the waist and one piece 58.5 cm (23 in) long for the neck. Machine the tapes to the raw edges of the apron in the appropriate positions.

(4) Turn in the raw edges of the apron all round and machine stitch into position, folding back the tapes and machining them at the same time.

(5) Neaten the ends of the ties by turning in a 6 mm (¼ in) double hem and machining in position.

7 *Bed valance, duvet cover and pillowcases made in co-ordinating fabrics*

11

THE BEDROOM

There are many different ways of making a bedroom look pretty and inviting, most of them inexpensive but very rewarding. Even a touch of luxury can be given to the smallest bedroom by the addition of one or two of the following items. Many of them also make delightful gifts for both the young and the not-so-young.

Bedspreads

A bedspread is often the focal point in a room and provides the most impact. It gives the largest expanse of colour and texture, and its choice, therefore, is of prime importance. The most successful bedcoverings are often those that combine originality with a discriminating choice of fabrics.

Simple throw-over bedspreads are easy to make. Many different effects can be achieved by the use of appliqué designs in firm fabrics. These are especially suited to children's and teenagers' rooms, and the theme can be carried through to the headboards, blinds or curtains to make an interesting overall design. Felt is the ideal material for appliqué as it does not fray and is therefore easy to use. But it does not wash. If using fabric that frays easily use a machine zigzag stitch to apply it to the face fabric, padding it slightly with a little synthetic wadding. Turning under the edges of an appliqué design gives a bulky finish.

Throw-over bedspreads can be decorated with braid, fringing or patchwork. For simple patchwork appliqué follow the instructions given for the hexagon shape given in Chapter 9 and apply to the bedspread with machine or handstitching.

Alternatively, English quilting can be worked on a throw-over bedspread (see instructions in Chapter 8); this is a most effective form of decoration, but of course is a more lengthy process.

Throw-over bedspread
Choose firm, mediumweight fabrics that are crease-resistant and that wash or dry clean easily. Remember, when choosing patterned fabric, that small or random match patterns are easier to handle than very large ones. Furnishing cottons, dupions, cotton lace, sailcloth and many of the man-made fabrics are all suitable for making attractive bedspreads.

Estimate the amount of fabric needed by taking the measurements over the bed when it is made up with the usual bedclothes and pillows. These are : A the top of the bed to the foot of the bed; B the width of the bed; C the height of the bed from the floor to the top of the bed (*fig. 201*). Usually, 6 m (6 yd) of 122 cm (48 in) wide fabric is sufficient for a standard length bed. This would be sufficient for a single or a medium sized double bed but more would be required for a king-sized bed, or when matching fabrics with large pattern repeats. Allow an extra 50 cm (18 in) if piping seams.
(1) Cut two widths of fabric 3 m (3 yd) long, cutting off all selvedges. Use one width for the central section, cut the

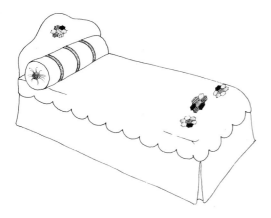

Fig. 198 *Patchwork appliqué on a bedspread*

Fig. 200 *Lace bedspread with scalloped edges*

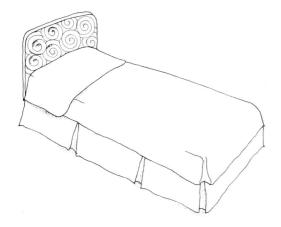

Fig. 199 *Quilting worked as surface decoration on a headboard*

other width in half lengthwise and join one to each side of the central section so that the seams are down each side of the bed and not in the middle. For a single bedspread the width of the centre section may need to be reduced to the width of the bed before the side sections are joined to it. Match any patterns carefully (*figs. 11 and 12*). The seams may be piped with matching or contrasting fabric, or covered with decorative braid. On patterned fabrics flat seams can be made and the edges neatened. If piping the seams, prepare and apply crossway strip and No. 3 piping cord to the central section before joining the side sections. When covering the seams with braid, make a flat seam with the wrong sides of the fabric together, so that the raw edges are covered on the right side of the bedspread by the braid. Alternatively, use a flat fell or a French seam (Chapter 4).

(2) Turn in both sides and bottom edge 1.3 cm (½ in). Mitre each corner, and make a 3.8 in(1½ in) hem. Slip stitch by hand. Alternatively, the corners at the foot of the bed can be rounded, using a large plate to obtain a curved shape. Cut one side of the bedspread first and then fold over to match the other side to it exactly.

(3) To make a lining for the bedspread cut out and seam the lining in the same way as the cover. With wrong sides together apply the lining to the cover matching seams. Lock stitch together along the seams (*fig. 17*). Turn in the lining and tack the bedspread 2.5 cm (1 in) from the edge all round. Slip stitch into position.

(4) Lay the bedspread on the bed. If using appliqué draw out the designs, cut them out and pin them to the bedspread, positioning them in the most effective way. Apply with machine zigzag, or stitch by hand. A thin layer of synthetic wadding sandwiched between the appliqué shape and the bedspread greatly enhances the finished result.

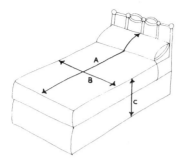

Fig. 201 *Taking the measurements of the bed*

Lace bedspread

White cotton lace can be used to make an attractive throw-over bedspread and looks effective over coloured blankets. This is obtainable in widths suitable for both single and double beds, so seams are unnecessary.

(1) Cut the bedspread to the required length and width and make a 2.5 cm (1 in) double hem at the top edge.

(2) If the lace has a suitable motif, cut round this to show off the pattern, perhaps making scalloped edges (*fig. 200*).

(3) Bind the raw edges with crossway strip or folded bias binding, or decorate with a suitable trimming.

Bed Valance

A valance is fitted over the base of the bed underneath the mattress and may be matched to fitted sheets and duvet covers. It is also used with throw-over bedspreads.

Choose polyester/cotton sheeting, dupion or other crease-resistant fabric. Economies can be made by using calico for the flat base section. The facings, however, must be made in the same fabric as the frill. The amount of fabric required depends on the size of the bed and style of frill used. (Usually 4–4.5 m (4–4½ yd) 122 cm (48 in) wide fabric is sufficient for a single or double bed.)

(1) Cut a piece of calico the size of the base plus 2.5 cm (1 in) turnings. Pin and tack a 1.3 cm (½ in) hem all round and machine.

(2) For a gathered frill allow one-and-a-half to two times the length of the frill round the base; for an inverted pleat at each of the bottom corners allow the length of the finished frill plus 20.5 cm (8 in) for each corner pleat.

(3) The depth of the frill can vary from 30.5 cm (12 in) to 35.5 cm (14 in), depending on the bed. Allow 7.5 cm (3 in) for turnings when cutting out.

(4) For the three facings cut three strips of fabric 15 cm (6 in) wide. Two must be the length of the bed base and one must be the width of the base. Allow 2.5 cm (1 in) turnings on each strip when cutting out.

(5) Pin the facing strips to the calico base and mitre the two corners. Remove the facing from the calico and machine the mitred corners leaving 1.3 cm (½ in) unstitched at each end (*figs. 28 and 29*).

(6) Join together the strips for the frill with 1.3 cm (½ in) turnings. Press seams open. Make a 1.3 cm (½ in) double hem at the two short sides of the frill and a 2.5 cm (1 in) double hem at the lower edge.

(7) Divide the calico base into six equal sections and mark these with tailor's chalk.

Fig. 202 *Appliquéd designs on a child's bedspread and headboard*

(8) For a gathered frill divide the length of the strip into six, and make two rows of running stitches 1.3 cm (½ in) from the top edge of each section. Draw up the gathering stitches and adjust so that they fit into each of the six sections marked on the calico base.

(9) With the wrong sides together pin and tack the frill to the base section. For pleated corners fold and arrange an inverted pleat at each bottom corner and tack into position with wrong sides facing.

(10) Cut and prepare the crossway strip for the piped edge. Apply this to the calico, pinning and tacking over the gathered edge, taking particular care not to stretch it.

(11) Pin and tack the facing to the frill over the piping, matching the mitred corners to the corners of the valance. Keep the right sides of the facing to the right side of the frill. Machine through all thicknesses along the two sides and the bottom edge of the valance.

(12) Lay the valance in position on the base of the bed so that it is flat. Turn in 1.3 cm (½ in) along the raw edges of the facing and pin and tack to the calico base. Remove the valance from the base and machine stitch using a large zigzag stitch (*fig. 204*).

Fig. 203 *Ideas for bedspreads*

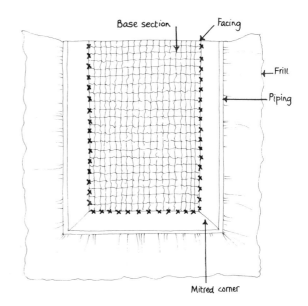

Fig. 204 *Valance facing stitched to the base using a large zigzag stitch*

Fig. 205 *Ideas for headboards*

Bedheads

An existing headboard can be covered with a loose cover in a plain or quilted fabric and fixed under the bottom of the headboard with ties. This is an inexpensive method of treating wooden or plastic covered headboards.

Matching box cushions can be made and suspended from a curtain pole attached to the wall.

Loose cover for a headboard

For a single size headboard (approx. 91.5 cm (36 in) wide by 61 cm (24 in) deep).

1.5 m (1¾ yd) 122 cm (48 in) wide fabric. Choose from furnishing cottons, dupions, repps, denim (or use ready-quilted fabric).

75 cm (1 yd) unbleached calico.

Synthetic wadding.

No. 3 piping cord.

(1) Cut out a paper pattern to the size of the headboard.

(2) Quilt a piece of fabric (Chapter 8) to the size of the pattern plus 2.5 cm (1 in) turnings for the front section. This can be worked by hand or machine. For the back section cut a piece of fabric to the same size. If this is quilted as well the cover will be reversible. Place the two sections together and notch round at intervals.

Fig. 206 *Neatening the ends of the crossway strip*

(3) If the headboard is more than 2.5 cm (1 in) thick it is best to insert a narrow gusset between the front and back sections. Piping can be used on the seams to give a tailored, professional finish. Alternatively, a pleated or gathered frill could be used to decorate the front section. If the headboard is 2.5 cm (1 in) or less in thickness it is not necessary to insert a gusset.

(4) For a gusset cut a piece of fabric on the straight grain long enough to insert round the two sides and the top of the cover. Cut and prepare crossway strip twice this length to pipe round both the front and back sections.

(5) Pin and tack the piping and crossway strip to the front and back sections, neatening the ends of the piping as in fig. 206.

(6) Pin and tack the gusset to both the front and back sections, matching notches. Machine into position and neaten seams.

(7) Turn up a 1.3 cm (½ in) double hem at the lower edges of the cover. Tack and machine.

(8) Sew six 25.5 cm (10 in) lengths of white tape in pairs to the back and front sections in three positions along the lower hem, and tie underneath the headboard when the cover is in place (*fig. 207*).

Fig. 207 *Tapes sewn to the lower edge of the cover*

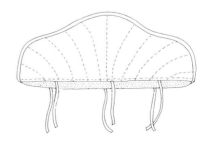

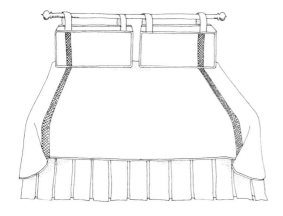

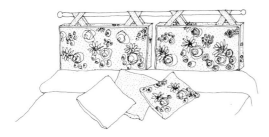

Fig. 208 *Box cushions used as a backrest*

Box cushions

Box cushions can be hung from curtain poles above beds or divans to make comfortable head or back rests (*fig. 208*).

Make the inner pad for these cushions from a rigid filling such as plastic or latex foam. Cut this to size and cover with calico before making the outer cover. When making covers for such cushions it is necessary to have a large opening to enable the rigid pad to be easily inserted; it is made at the back of the cushion and should extend round the sides for 5–10 cm (2–4 in). This measurement is determined by the depth of the welt (*fig. 95*). When measuring and cutting out the fabric remember to take the exact measurements of the pad, for this is rigid, and add 1.3 cm (½ in) turnings all round (1.9 cm (¾ in) if the fabric frays easily).

(1) Prepare a cutting plan to estimate the amount of fabric required (*fig. 209*).

(2) Cut out the fabric following the plan, and allow 1.3 cm (½ in) turnings on all pieces. Centralize any pattern there may be.

(3) With right sides facing, tack the front and back sections together to hold the two pieces firmly in position (*fig. 210*).

(4) Pin in each welt separately, placing right sides together. Tack 2.5 cm (1 in) from the edge of the fabric and 2.5 cm (1 in) from the edge of the welt (*fig. 210*). Tack and machine the corner seams of the welt to within 1.3 cm (½ in) of each edge, taking 1.3 cm (½ in) turnings. Press the four corner seams open.

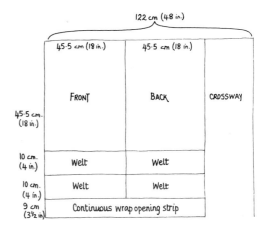

Fig. 209 *Cutting plan for a box cushion*

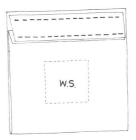

Fig. 210 *Pinning in the welt on a box cushion*

109

(5) Apply crossway strip and piping cord to the front and back sections of the cover, inserting it between the welt and the front and back sections (*fig. 211*). Pin and tack, clipping corners. Machine round the front section using a zipper foot and stitching as closely as possible to the piping cord.

(6) For the loops cut a strip of fabric on the straight grain 15 cm (6 in) wide, and long enough to fit round the curtain pole (approx. 28–38 cm (11–15 in). Fold in half lengthwise with right sides facing. Pin and tack a 1.3 cm (½ in) seam and machine in position (*fig. 212*). Trim seam and neaten edges. Turn to the right sides and press in position having the seam at the back as in fig. 213. Mark positions for loops on the back section of the cover. Carefully unpick the tacking stitches at these points and pin and tack the loops in position on top of the piping cord, inserting the loop between the front and back sections of the cover. Re-tack.

(7) Machine stitch the seams of the back section, leaving the opening at the back unstitched.

(8) Take out all the tacking stitches and turn the cushion cover to the right side.

(9) Make a continuous wrap opening along the back and side seams (Chapter 7), or insert the pad and slip stitch the opening together.

Fig. 211 *Inserting the piping cord and crossway strip between the welt and the back section*

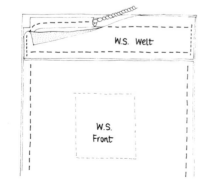

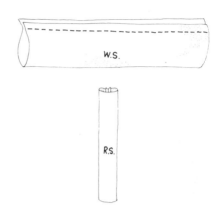

Figs. 212 and 213 *Making a loop*

Bed Canopies and Drapes

Elegant four poster beds can be made from wooden kits bought ready to assemble at home. They can also be made using standard curtain poles and ring fittings. Screw the upright poles into the base of the bed to hold them firmly into position (*fig. 214*) and fix the cross poles with brackets for added strength. Alternatively, use the special rods, brackets and supports available from some curtain track manufacturers.

Drape the four poster with curtains, pelmets and valances made in exactly the same way as window curtains (Chapters 5 and 6). Keep the fabrics as light as possible. Choose from polyester/cotton sheeting to match the bed linen, light furnishing cottons, or dainty man-made voiles and laces that are easy to wash (*fig. 216*).

A more permanent fitting for a four poster bed can be made by screwing wooden battens to the ceiling onto which a hardboard facing may be attached. A curtain track can be fixed to the battens, and the valance or pelmet attached with touch-and-close fastening (Velcro) (*fig. 217*).

A small canopy can be made at the head of the bed by fixing wooden battens to the ceiling or walls and then attaching a valance rod to it. Make and attach the canopy in exactly the same way as a valance (Chapter 6).

Fig. 214 *Four poster made from standard curtain poles and fittings*

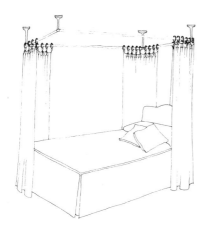

Fig. 215 *Do-it-yourself four poster made using copper tubing*

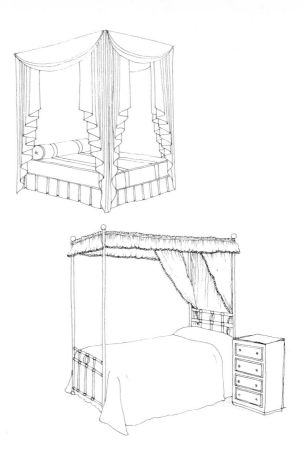

Fig. 216 *Drape four poster beds with light washable fabrics*

Position the battens so that they extend approximately 10 cm (4 in) at each side of the bed and extend them out from the wall approximately 15—23 cm (6—9 in). A straight curtain may be used at the back of the bed, being fixed to the same batten as the valance rod (*fig. 219*).

A 'coronet' is another attractive way of treating a bed and is easily made by using a flexible track fixed to battens on the wall. A decorative curtain rod can be fixed at right angles to the wall over the centre of the bed. The curtains can be hung from the pole and held back at the sides of the bed with decorative or metal tie-backs (*figs. 220 and 221*).

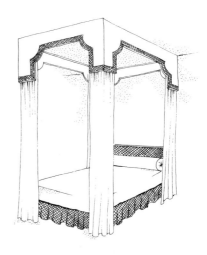

Fig. 217 *Four poster bed using battens fixed to the ceiling and a pelmet attached with touch-and-close fastening (Velcro)*

111

Fig. 218 *Draping a child's cot*

Fig. 220 *Coronet for a bed using a flexible track*

Fig. 219 *A canopy at the head of the bed fixed to the ceiling with wooden battens*

Fig. 221 *A curtain rod fixed at right angles to the wall over the centre of the bed*

Dressing Table Cover

A draped dressing table makes an attractive feature in a feminine bedroom. Use a white-wood kidney-shaped dressing table with a plate glass top, or a small chest of drawers with a knee hole and a table top extending over the front and side edges. Or improvise by using plain wooden shelves fixed to the wall (*fig. 222*).

A light plastic or flexible curtain track should be fixed underneath the table top and curved to its shape. From this hang a pair of curtains which meet at the centre front. The top of the table is covered with fabric and a small pelmet attached to cover the headings of the curtains.

Making the curtains
(1) The curtains for this type of dressing table can be lined or unlined depending on the fabric chosen. Follow the instructions for making curtains in Chapter 5.
(2) For flimsy fabrics allow two to three times the length of the curtain track, or enough fullness to conceal the woodwork underneath. For furnishing cottons, one-and-a-half to twice the width of the track is sufficient.

Fig. 222 *A wooden shelf made into an attractive dressing table*

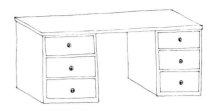

Fig. 223 *Covering a kneehole desk*

(3) Make the curtains to finish 1.3 cm (½ in) from the floor, and have an overlap at the centre front. They can be drawn back for easy access to storage space and drawers. Use a simple gathered heading at the top of the curtains, for this will be covered by the pelmet.

Covering the table top

(1) Make a paper pattern of the top of the table by drawing round the plate glass top. From this cut one piece of bonded interfacing (Vilene). Cut out the fabric and the lining using the paper pattern, cutting both 2.5 cm (1 in) larger all round to allow for turnings. Centralize any pattern there may be.

(2) Place the interfacing to the wrong side of the cover fabric and tack. Turn over the 2.5 cm (1 in) seam allowance to the wrong side, and herringbone stitch in position (*fig. 225*).

(3) Apply the lining to the wrong side of the top cover turning in 2.5 cm (1 in) all round. Slip stitch into position.

The fabric for the table top could be machine or hand quilted instead of interlined with Vilene, giving an attractive padded effect to

Fig. 224 *Covering a kidney-shaped dressing table*

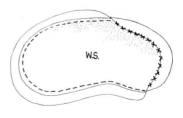

Fig. 225 *Applying the interfacing to the face fabric*

113

Fig. 226 *Loose covers for a table, stool and a box*

the top of the table. Use a thin layer of synthetic wadding and a piece of muslin when quilting the face fabric. Protect the top with a piece of plate glass, which can be obtained cut to size.

The pelmet
(1) Make the pelmet following the instructions given in Chapter 6 using heavyweight bonded interfacing (Vilene) as a foundation instead of buckram, as this is washable.
(2) Do not apply tape to the top edge of the pelmet but pin it in position to the cover of the dressing table top. Start at the centre front, then slip stitch neatly in place. This method of fixing prevents dust collecting in the pockets at the top edge of the pelmet.
(3) Do not make the pelmet for a dressing table too deep, or it will interfere with the smooth working of the drawers. Usually, a depth of 10—15 cm (4—6 in) is sufficient. When plain fabrics are used, the pelmet can be decorated with embroidery, patchwork or quilting.

Cover for a box or stool
A simple loose cover for a table, box, trunk or stool can be made in the following way. It is a useful method of dressing up a utilitarian piece of furniture and matching it to other soft furnishings (*fig. 226*). Choose firmly

woven furnishing cottons that wash well, remembering to pre-shrink the piping cord before use. (Boil it for five minutes and let it dry thoroughly.)
(1) Make a paper pattern of the top of the table or stool and add 1.3 cm (½ in) turnings. To estimate the amount of fabric needed take the necessary measurements and make a cutting plan. Ensure that the selvedge runs down the fabric from the top to the bottom on both the skirt and the welt sections.
(2) Cut out the fabric, allowing 1.3 cm (½ in) turnings on all sections. For a square or rectangular table, box or stool, cut four welts of equal depth (usually 7.5—10 cm (3—4 in), by the length of the sides, plus 1.3 cm (½ in) turnings.
(3) Join the four welt sections together along the short sides using 1.3 cm (½ in) turnings. Press seams open.

Fig. 227 *Tacking the welt sections to the top section*

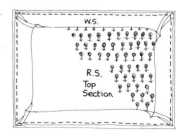

8 *A coronet for a bed. The bed valance matches the lining of the drapes*

(i)

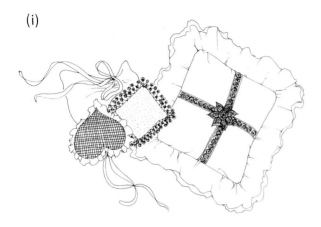

(4) Apply piping and crossway strip round the right side of the table top section, as in fig. 57.
(5) With right sides facing apply the welt sections to the top section, matching corners carefully. Tack and machine into position (*fig. 227*).
(6) Apply piping cord and crossway strip to the lower edges of the welt sections.
(7) Prepare and make the skirt section as for a loose cover frill (Chapter 7), making a 1.3 cm (½ in) double hem at the lower edge and joining widths of fabric together if necessary to obtain the required amount of fulness.
(8) Apply the skirt section to the piped edge of the welt with right sides facing, following the instructions in Chapter 7.

Herb and Boudoir Cushions

Pretty, decorative 'boudoir' cushions can be made in all shapes and sizes and filled with sweet scented herbs and lavender. Use marjoram, meadowsweet, lemon verbena, rosemary, thyme, hops and rosebuds. Herb pillows are a pleasant way of inducing sleep, they make delightful gifts and add a touch of luxury to the bedroom.

Choose satins, silks, fine cottons, lace and organdie for best effects, or match the cushions to other bed linen using polyester/cotton

(ii)

(iii)

(iv)

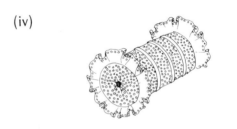

Fig. 228 *Some ideas for cushions*
(i) *Use of a double frill*
(ii) *Pintucking detail on fine cotton fabric*
(iii) *Cushions made in shell shapes using English quilting as surface decoration*
(iv) *Bolster cushion lavishly decorated*

sheeting or light furnishing cottons with small designs. Trim the cushions lavishly with broderie anglaise, lace or frills, or use pin tucking or quilting as surface decoration (*fig. 228*).

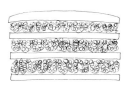

Fig. 229 *Making a pad for a cushion using layers of synthetic wadding and herbs*

Heart-shaped cushion

(1) Cut out a paper pattern of a heart to the size required and add 1.3 cm (½ in) turnings. Remember that the filling will take up some of the fabric, so cut the pattern slightly larger to allow for this. Use simple shapes such as hearts, triangles, diamonds and shells.

(2) Make an inner pad to the same shape using fine lawn or muslin and synthetic wadding as a filling. Sprinkle the herbs or lavender between three or four layers of wadding to make a sandwich (*fig. 229*). Oversew round the edges to hold the layers in place, and slip it into the inner case and oversew the opening. This method of filling gives the cushion a smooth appearance when finished and the herbs do not show through the face fabric.

(3) Make the outer cover for the cushion following the instructions in Chapter 7, but instead of piping, insert broderie anglaise, lace or frills to give it a luxurious look. Sew up the opening with a slip-stitch.

Padded Coat Hanger

Wooden coat hanger.
Cotton lawn, dress fabric or light furnishing cotton (50 cm, 18 in, covers four hangers approximately 43 cm, 17 in, long).
Synthetic wadding.
Bump or domette.

(1) Cut a strip of fabric for the cover 45.5 cm (18 in) by 1.3 cm (½ in) wide to bind the metal hook. Fold in and press 3 mm ($\frac{1}{8}$ in) along one long side of the strip. Bind the hook with the strip of fabric, overlapping it so that the raw edges are enclosed. Apply a little adhesive to the metal to hold it firmly in place. Wind the strip round the hanger at the bottom of the hook and secure with a few stitches (*fig. 231*).

(2) Bind the hanger with a strip of bump or domette (or other soft fabric). Cut a piece approximately 5 cm (2 in) wide and two-and-a-half times the length of the hanger. Use a little adhesive on the wooden part of the hanger to secure it firmly. Finish with a few stitches to hold it in place (*fig. 232*).

Fig. 230 *Coat hangers make attractive accessories*

Fig. 231 *Binding the hook of a wooden coat hanger*

117

Fig. 232 *Binding the hanger with a strip of bump*

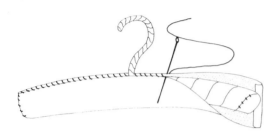

Fig. 233 *Sewing the wadding in place*

Fig. 234 *Finding the centre of the cover fabric*

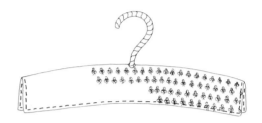

Fig. 235 *Slipping the cover fabric over the hanger*

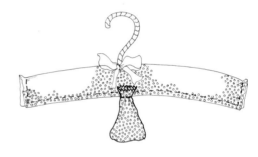

Fig. 236 *The cover and lavender bag stitched in position*

(3) Cut a piece of synthetic wadding the length of the hanger plus 2.5 cm (1 in) and 45.5. cm (18 in) x 10 cm (4 in) wide. Fold this round the hanger turning in each end 1.3 cm (½ in) and oversew along the top edge (*fig. 233*).

(4) Cut a piece of fabric 48.5 cm (19 in) x 18 cm (7 in) for the cover. Turn in a 6 mm (¼ in) hem on to the wrong side of the fabric on all sides. Machine stitch in position and press.

(5) Find the centre of the fabric by folding first in half and then in quarters. Make a hole by snipping off the corner as in fig. 234. Slip the cover over the hanger with the hook going through the hole (*fig. 235*).

(6) Pin the machined edges together and sew with a running stitch using double thread, gathering where necessary to take in any fullness. This is particularly necessary at the two ends of the hanger (*fig. 236*). Tie a bow of satin ribbon 6 mm (¼ in) wide round the hook.

(7) Make a lavender bag following the instructions given below and attach securely with a few stab stitches (*fig. 236*). Alternatively, make a small sachet and hang round the hanger with satin ribbon (*fig. 237*).

Lavender Bags and Pot Pourri Sachets

Dry the lavender by hanging in bunches upside down with a paper bag tied round the flowers. The flowers when dry will then fall into the paper bag. Do not use a plastic bag as this will not allow the air to circulate.

Fig. 237 *Small sachets filled with pot pourri or lavender*

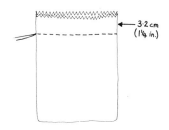

Fig. 238 *Making a lavender bag*

(1) Cut two pieces of fabric 10 cm (4 in) x 7.5 cm (3 in) to match the hanger. With right sides together tack and machine the two sides and the lower edge allowing 6 mm (¼ in) turnings. Snip corners and turn the right sides out.

(2) Cut along the top edge of the bag with pinking shears.

(3) Make a row of running stitches round the edge of the bag 3.2 cm (1¼ in) from the top of the bag (*fig. 238*).

(4) Fill the bag with dried lavender flowers or pot pourri and draw up running stitches to enclose. Secure with a few stitches.

(5) Tie a small piece of satin ribbon 6 mm (¼ in) wide round the top of the lavender bag and sew to the hanger as in fig. 236.

(6) Alternatively, small sachets can be made using simple shapes such as hearts, circles, ovals or squares. Fill them with lavender or pot pourri and hang them from hangers with pieces of satin ribbon (*fig. 237*).

Duvet Cover

Duvet covers are easily made from wide width polyester/cotton sheeting or other easy care lightweight fabrics. If possible, choose wide width fabrics as these need less seaming.

The duvet cover should be made slightly larger than the duvet itself so that it does not constrict the duvet when it is in use. Make an opening along the top edge of the cover and finish it with press studs, Velcro or a zip fastener. Alternatively, a housewife flap can be made as for a pillowcase (see next section).

For a single size duvet, 137 x 190.5 cm (54 x 75 in), allow approximately 3 m (3½ yd) of 228 cm (90 in) wide fabric. For a double size, 205.5 x 198 cm (81 x 78 in) allow 4.2 metres (4½ yd). The amount of fabric needed to make a duvet cover obviously depends on the size of the duvet and the width of the fabric. The measurements should be checked carefully before cutting out the fabric as duvet sizes vary considerably.

(1) Cut out the fabric in one of the following ways depending on the width of the fabric available:

(a) Twice the length of the duvet plus 5 cm (2 in) x the width of the duvet plus 5 cm (2 in).

(b) Twice the width of the duvet plus 5 cm (2 in) x the length of the duvet plus 5 cm (2 in).

(c) Two separate pieces of fabric the length of the duvet plus 5 cm (2 in) x the width of the duvet plus 5 cm (2 in).

119

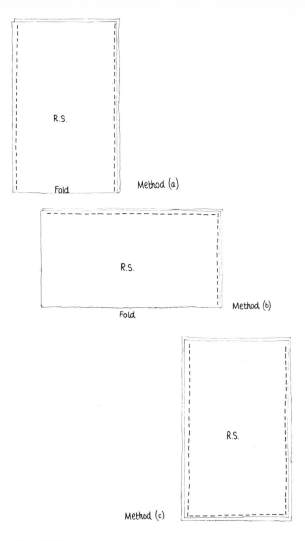

Fig. 239 *Three methods of cutting and sewing a duvet*

(2) For methods (a) and (b) fold the fabric in half widthwise or lengthwise with wrong sides facing (*fig. 239*). Tack and machine the cover using French seams.

(3) For method (c) pin and tack the two sections together with wrong sides facing and make French seams round the three sides (*fig. 239*).

(4) At the opening edge at the top of the duvet, make a 1.3 cm (½ in) double hem and apply touch-and-close fastening (Velcro), press studs or a zip fastener. Alternatively, make a housewife flap as for a pillowcase (see next section).

Pillowcases

Pillowcases can be made to match duvet covers or sheets and are easy to make in either a plain or a frilled style. They can be decorated with broderie anglaise or other trimmings, or can have single or double frills made in matching or co-ordinating fabric (*fig. 240*).

Pillows vary in size, so it is necessary to measure them carefully to estimate the amount of fabric needed. Make a pillowcase to fit loosely so that it does not constrict the pillow in use.

Plain pillowcases with housewife flap (51 x 76 cm, 20 x 30 in)

These can be made by folding one long strip of fabric, or by using separate sections, the method chosen depending on the fabric available.

(1) Cut a piece of fabric 53.5 cm x 173 cm (21 x 68 in).

(2) Pin and tack a 1.3 cm (½ in) double hem along one short side. On the other short side turn over 6 mm (¼ in) to the wrong side and then 2.5 cm (1 in) to make a hem. Pin and tack. Machine both hems in position.

(3) Fold the fabric as in fig. 245, enclosing the short side with the narrow hem for 15 cm (6 in), and taking the other short side to meet the fold.

(4) Pin and tack along the two long sides to form the pillowcase, having wrong sides together (*fig. 245*). Machine and trim seams to 3 mm ($\frac{1}{8}$ in). Turn the pillowcase to the wrong sides and complete the French seam (*fig. 246*). Turn the pillowcase and the flap to the right sides and press.

Alternatively, this type of pillowcase can be made using two sections if it is more convenient.

(1) Cut out one section 53.5 x 96.5 cm (21 x 38 in) for the front section and one piece 51 x 81.5 cm (20 x 32 in) for the back section.

120

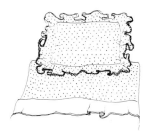

Fig. 240 *Pillowcase with a wide gathered frill and machine scalloping*

Fig. 241 *Broderie anglaise used to trim pillowcase and duvet cover*

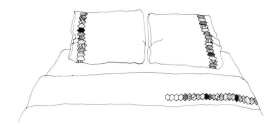

Fig. 242 *Patchwork motifs used to decorate pillowcases and sheet*

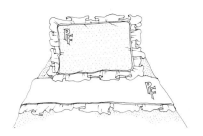

Fig. 243 *Gathered frill and appliquéd initials used to decorate pillowcase and sheet*

(2) Pin and tack a 2.5 cm (1 in) double hem along one short side of the front section. Machine. On the one short side of the back section tack and machine a 1.3 cm (½ in) double hem.

(3) With wrong sides facing fold in the flap on the front section as in fig. 247 and make a French seam round the three sides of the pillowcase.

Pillowcase with a frill and housewife flap

(1) Cut one piece of fabric 53.5 x 78.5 cm (21 x 31 in) for the front section, another piece 53.5 x 81.5 cm (21 x 32 in) for the back section, and one piece 53.5 x 15 cm (21 x 6 in) for the flap.

(2) Pin and tack a 6 mm (¼ in) double hem along one long side of the flap section. Machine.

(3) On the back section turn under 6 mm (¼ in) and then fold over 3.8 cm (1½ in) to make a hem. Tack and machine.

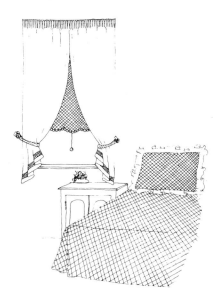

Fig. 244 *Matching pillowcase and bedspread*

121

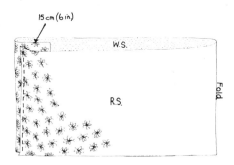

Fig. 245 *Folding the strip of fabric to enclose the 15 cm (6 in) flap*

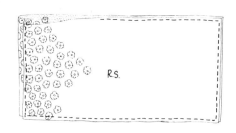

Fig. 247 *Assembling the pillowcase using two sections*

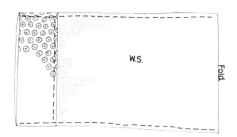

Fig. 246 *The French seam completed on the wrong side of the pillowcase*

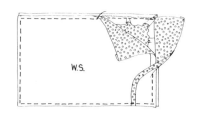

Fig. 248 *Assembling the pillowcase and stitching in position*

(4) Make a gathered frill for application to the front section. Tack and machine this into position. Follow the instructions for making frills in Chapter 4. Alternatively, make a frill using machine scalloping or apply a trimming such as broderie anglaise or lace.

(5) Apply the back section to the front section with right sides together keeping the hem 1.3 cm (½ in) from the raw edges of the top section (*fig. 248*).

(6) Apply the right side of the flap to the wrong side of the back section as in fig. 248. Pin and tack round all four sides of the pillowcase taking care not to stitch in the hem of the back section at the opening end of the pillowcase. Machine stitch in position and neaten seams.

(7) Turn the pillowcase and flap opening to the right sides and press.

Photograph Frames

Attractive frames can be made for photographs of all sizes, and are very acceptable gifts. Single and double photograph frames can be made following the instructions below, and can be adapted to any size of photograph.

Choose closely woven fabrics made from natural fibres to cover the frame because these fold well and are easy to use. Dress cottons and lightweight furnishing cottons, linen or silk are all suitable fabrics. With fine fabrics such as silk, a very thin layer of synthetic wadding can be placed behind the fabric to give a padded look. Man-made fibres are more difficult to handle than ones made from natural fibres; they do not fold well as they are rather springy.

9 *Quilted bedspread matches the tablecloths and bed valance made in co-ordinating fabrics*

Fig. 249 *Fabric covered photograph frames*

Photograph frame 16.5 x 12.5 cm (6½ x 5 in) (fig. 249).

Fabric for cover.
Stiff card.
Acetate film.
Adhesive.

(1) Cut out three pieces of card 16.5 x 12.5 cm (6½ x 5 in) and mark them 'front', 'middle', and 'back'.

(2) In the middle of the 'front' piece of card, cut out a 'window' 2.5 cm (1 in) in from the edge using a craft knife or a very sharp pair of scissors, being particularly careful to get a sharp cut at the four corners (*fig. 250*).

(3) On the piece of card marked 'back' score a line with a sharp knife 5 cm (2 in) down from the top edge from side to side (*fig. 251*).

(4) Cut out three pieces of fabric 21.5 x 18 cm (8½ x 7 in) to cover the card.

(5) Place one piece of fabric right side down on the table and lay the back section on top with the scored side uppermost. Mitre the corner as in fig. 251, cutting off part of the mitre as shown to make the corner less bulky. Secure the fabric firmly in place with adhesive. Cut a piece of good quality writing or typing paper to the size of the back section and apply to the wrong side of the card over the raw edges of the fabric.

124

(6) Cover the middle section with fabric and paper in the same way as the back section. Place the middle and back sections together with paper sides facing and apply adhesive from the top edge down to the score line for 5 cm (2 in).

(7) Apply the cover fabric to the front section in the same way as for the back section, but when the outer edges have been secured with adhesive cut out a small rectangle in the middle of the fabric. Trim and fold back as in fig. 253. Secure firmly in place with adhesive.

(8) Apply the front section to the middle and back sections carefully spreading the glue in a 6 mm (¼ in) strip round the two sides and bottom edges of the middle section. Leave the top edge open so that the photograph can be inserted.

Fig. 250 *The 'front' piece of card cut out and ready to be covered*

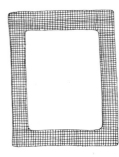

Fig. 251 *Mitring a corner on the 'back' section; the score line is marked 5 cm (2 in) from the top edge*

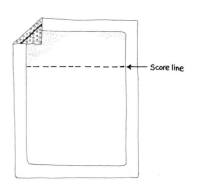

Score line

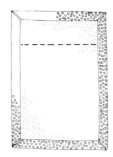

Fig. 252 *The corners mitred and secured with adhesive on the back section*

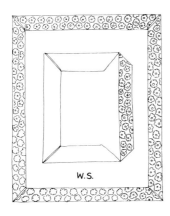

Fig. 253 *Folding back and securing the fabric on the front section*

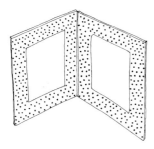

Fig. 254 *Double photograph frame covered in fabric*

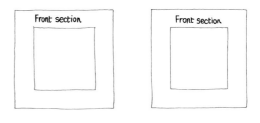

Fig. 255 *Cutting out the card for the front sections*

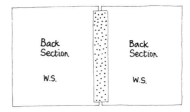

Fig. 256 *Fixing the two back sections together*

(9) Cut a piece of acetate film slightly smaller than the size of the frame and insert it between the front and middle sections to protect the photograph.

Double Photograph Frame 25.5 x 12.5 cm (10 x 5 in) (fig. 254)
(1) Cut four pieces of card 12.5 x 12.5 cm (5 x 5 in).
(2) On two pieces of the card measure 2.5 cm (1 in) from each edge and cut out a window 7.5 x 7.5 cm (3 x 3 in) (*fig. 255*). Cut two pieces of cover fabric 15 x 15 cm (6 x 6 in) and lay the pieces of card on the fabric with right sides facing. Fold over the fabric at the outer edges and mitre each corner as in fig. 251. Secure to the card with adhesive; cut out the fabric in the middle of the window, trim and fold back the fabric as in fig. 253.

(3) Cut a strip of cover fabric 1.9 cm (¾ in) wide x 12.5 cm (5 in) long, and with this join the two plain pieces of card together using adhesive. Leave a gap of 6 mm (¼ in) between the two pieces of card (*fig. 256*).

(4) Cut a piece of cover fabric 15 cm (6 in) x 29 cm (11½ in). Place the back sections on to the wrong side of the fabric and fold over the edges 1.3 cm (½ in). Mitre each corner as in fig. 251, and secure firmly with adhesive (*fig. 257*).

(5) Place the two front window sections to the wrong side of the back section (*fig. 258*). Apply adhesive in a 6 mm (¼ in) strip round the two sides and bottom edges leaving the top edges open for insertion of the photographs.

(6) Cut two pieces of acetate film slightly smaller than the size of the frames and insert them between the front and back sections to protect the photograph.

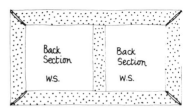

Fig. 257 *Covering the back sections with fabric*

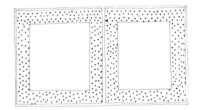

Fig. 258 *Fixing the front 'window' sections to the wrong side of the back section*

12

THE BATHROOM

Pretty accessories can be made for the bathroom in matching or co-ordinating fabrics. Some of the following ideas also make practical gifts and may be adapted for use in other rooms in the home.

Fig. 259 *Bath hat*

Bath and Shower Hats

Choose polyester/cotton or fine lawn fabric, as these are quick-drying. Use a waterproof fabric such as shower curtain material for the linings.

50 cm (18 in) 91.5 cm (36 in) wide fabric makes two hats 45.5 cm (18 in) in diameter.
50 cm (18 in) waterproof fabric.
153 cm (60 in) nylon lace trimming.
75 cm (27 in) hat elastic.

(1) Make a paper pattern of a circle 45.5 cm (18 in) in diameter. (The size of the hat can be varied by 5—7.5 cm (2—3 in) to make smaller or larger hats.)

(2) Using the paper pattern cut out a circle of both the cover fabric and the waterproof fabric 45.5 cm (18 in) in diameter (*fig. 260*).

(3) Place the shower fabric to the wrong side of the cover fabric and tack together round the outer edges (*fig. 261*).

(4) Tack the trimming to the right side of the cover fabric close to the edge, making sure that both the lining and the cover fabric are enclosed (*fig. 261*). Overlap the two ends of the trimming. Machine the trimming in place, using a small zigzag stitch. Cut away the surplus fabric as close as possible to the lace.

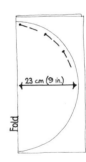

Fig. 260 *Cutting out the fabric for a bath hat*

(5) Make a casing for the elastic by making a tacking line 1.3 cm (½ in) from the outer edge. Machine along this line. Work another row of machine stitching 6 mm (¼ in) from the first line (*fig. 262*).

(6) Make a small hole in the casing in the shower fabric only, and thread the hat elastic through using a small safety pin (*fig. 262*). Draw up the elastic to fit, and knot to hold it securely in place.

Fig. 261 *Tacking the trimming to the right side of the hat*

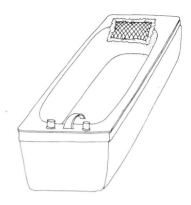

Fig. 263 *Bath cushion in position*

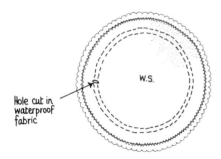

Hole cut in waterproof fabric

Fig. 262 *Making a casing for the elastic*

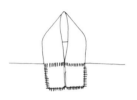

Fig. 264 *Making loops of fabric to attach to the cushion pad*

Bath Cushion

To make this cushion for the bath either make a pad to the size required using plastic foam for the filling, or buy a ready-made bath cushion pad from a major department store or chain store chemist.

Choose a quick-drying fabric for the cover such as polyester/cotton, nylon or seersucker. Use a waterproof lining or shower curtain fabric to make the pad and attach two loops of fabric to the pad through which to insert two small suction caps (*figs. 264 and 265*).

(1) For a pad 29 x 18 cm (11½ x 7 in) cut the cover fabric as follows:
Front section — 31.5 x 20.5 cm (12½ x 8 in)
Back section 1 — 31.5 x 7.5 cm (12½ x 3 in)
Back section 2 — 31.5 x 15 cm (12½ x 6 in)

Fig. 265 *Fixing the cushion to the bath using suction caps*

(2) On one long side of each of the two back sections turn over the raw edge and fold in a 1.3 cm (½ in) hem. Tack and machine stitch (*fig. 266*).

(3) On the right side of the front section tack and machine a trimming or a gathered or pleated frill to the outer edge (*fig. 267*).

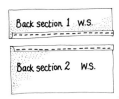

Fig. 266   *Hems worked on the back sections*

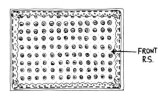

Fig. 267   *Applying the trimming to the front section*

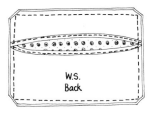

Fig. 268   *Assembling the cushion cover, overlapping the hems on the back sections*

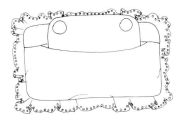

Fig. 269   *Back view of a bath cushion using a ready made plastic pad*

(4)   With right sides facing place back section 1 to the front section and pin in position; then apply back section 2 to the front section, overlapping the hems as in fig. 268. Tack the sections in position enclosing the trimming, and machine stitch all round. Clip the corners, neaten the edges and turn the cushion cover to the right side. Attach to the bath using the suction caps (*fig. 269*).

Tissue Box Cover

Tissue boxes look attractive when given a tailored cover to match other accessories such as shower caps, bath cushions, padded hangers and so on. They look equally well in the kitchen or cloakroom, besides the bathroom or bedroom, and make charming gifts when matched up in this way (*fig. 270*).

As tissue boxes vary slightly in size it is advisable to tailor the cover to a well known make.

Choose polyester/cotton fabrics, dress or light furnishing cottons. Avoid fabrics that are very springy as these are difficult to handle successfully.

Tissue box 38 x 25.5 cm (15 x 10 in).
(1)   Take the measurements of the tissue box as in fig. 271 to estimate the amount of fabric needed.
(2)   Cut a piece of fabric to this measurement plus 2.5 cm (1 in) for turnings allowances, i.e. 40.5 x 28 cm (16 x 11 in).
(3)   Place the fabric right side down over the tissue box and anchor it in place with pins. Pin and tack the fabric at each corner as in fig. 272 taking care to tack with the grain of the fabric and at right angles to the top of the box. Machine stitch each corner and trim the seams to 6 mm (¼ in).
(4)   Turn up the lower edge making a 1.3 cm (½ in) hem and apply a trimming or frill round this edge using a small machine zigzag stitch.

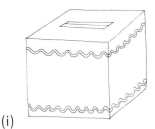

(i)

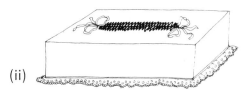

(ii)

Fig. 270 *Tailored covers for tissue boxes*
(i) Tissue box with a bound buttonhole
(ii) Tissue box with a machine worked
buttonhole

(5) Place the cover on the tissue box and mark the position for the opening with a tacking line (*fig. 273*). On a small box make the opening approximately 6.4—7.5 cm (2½—3 in) long and on a larger box approximately 14—15 cm (5½ —6 in) long.

(6) Finish the opening as for a buttonhole. Either make a machine buttonhole with a close zigzag stitch or face the opening as in a bound buttonhole, as follows:

(a) Cut a piece of fabric for the facing approximately the size of the top of the box (11.5 x 24 cm) (4½ x 9½ in). Lay this with right sides facing, over the marked position for the opening. Mark this position through to the facing with tacking stitches (*fig. 274*).

(b) Machine stitch round the tacking line keeping 6 mm (¼ in) away from it and having right angled corners as in fig. 275.

(c) Cut along the tacking line with a sharp pair of scissors to within 6 mm (¼ in) of each end, cutting into the corners diagonally as in fig. 276.

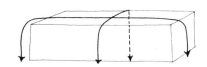

Fig. 271 *Estimating the amount of fabric*

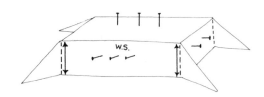

Fig. 272 *Tacking the corners of the cover*

Fig. 273 *Marking the position for the opening at the top of the box*

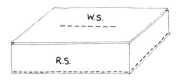

Fig. 274 *Marking the opening on the facing*

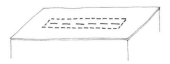

Fig. 275 *Machining the fabric 6 mm (¼ in) away from the tacking line*

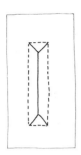

Fig. 276 *Cutting the fabric diagonally into the corners*

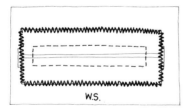

W.S.

Fig. 277 *Making an inverted pleat on the wrong side of the cover*

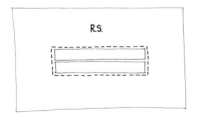

R.S.

Fig. 278 *Machining the opening on the right side*

(d) Take the facing through to the wrong side of the cover and fold the fabric so that 6 mm (¼ in) shows on the right side, forming an inverted pleat on the wrong side (*fig. 277*).

(e) Tack the facing in position and machine stitch round the opening on the right side to give the opening strength (*fig. 278*). Trim off the surplus fabric on the wrong side of the opening and neaten the edges (*fig. 277*).

Toilet Bag

Choose polyester/cotton fabric for the outer cover and use a waterproof lining such as shower curtain fabric.

Toilet bag 30.5 x 24 cm (12 x 9½ in)

(1) Cut a piece of cover fabric and a piece of waterproof fabric each 71 x 28 cm (28 x 11 in).

(2) Place the waterproof fabric to the wrong side of the cover fabric, fold in half with the right sides of the fabric outside and tack along both side edges (*fig. 280*). Make French seams at the two side edges.

Fig. 279 *Toilet bag with waterproof lining*

131

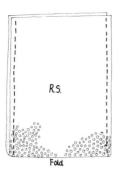

Fig. 280 *Making French seams at each side of the toilet bag*

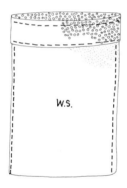

Fig. 281 *Hem machine stitched into position*

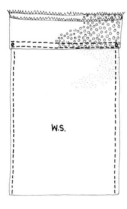

Fig. 282 *Making a casing with two rows of machine stitch*

(3) Turn over the top edge first 6 mm (¼ in) and then 3.8 cm (1½ in) and tack the hem in position. Work a line of tacking stitches round the top edge of the bag. Machine stitch the hem in position and make a casing by working another row of machine stitching 1.9 cm (¾ in) above the first (*fig. 281*).

(4) Make four small holes in the casing, two at each side edge, and neaten with buttonhole stitch. Thread approximately 137 cm (54 in) of narrow nylon cord through the casing, taking it round twice. Leave a large loop at each side so that it pulls up easily.

(5) A lace trimming can be applied to the top edge of the bag using a small machine zigzag stitch.

Make-up Bag

(1) Cut out a piece of machine-or hand-quilted fabric 23 x 40.5 cm (9 x 16 in) (Chapter 8) and a piece of waterproof lining to the same measurement.

(2) Place the waterproof lining fabric to the wrong side of the quilted fabric and tack round the outer edges to hold them in position.

(3) Fold in half lengthwise and cut off the corner, making a curved edge as in fig. 284.

Fig. 283 *Make-up bags*

10 *The patterns on the wallpaper and fabric used for curtains, cushions and tablecloth echo each other*

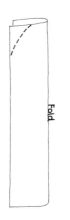

Fold

Fig. 284 *Cutting a curved edge*

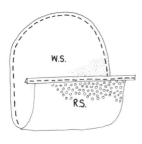

W.S.

R.S.

Fig. 285 *Finishing the short side with bias binding*

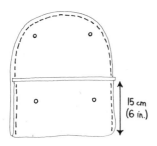

15 cm
(6 in.)

Fig. 286 *Folding the fabric up 15 cm (6 in) and machining into position*

(4) Bind the other short side with bias binding, tacking and machining the binding to the right side of the bag. Turn over and hem stitch to the waterproof lining (*fig. 285*).

(5) Fold up the front edge of the bag 15 cm (6 in) and pin, tack and machine into position (*fig. 286*).

(6) Pin, tack and machine bias binding to the front side of the bag. Turn over and hem stitch to the back of the bag.

(7) Attach two snap fasteners to the front of the bag in the positions shown in fig. 286.

Wastepaper Bin or Bathroom Tidy

Use small cans or large drum shaped tins to make decorative wastepaper bins and useful tidies for cotton wool, pencils, soaps and so forth. These are useful additions to bedrooms, kitchens, studies or playrooms and take very little fabric. If using food cans make sure there are no rough edges at the top. Paint the inside with quick drying enamel or gloss paint and allow to dry thoroughly before use.

(1) Measure the depth of the bin and its circumference to estimate the amount of fabric required (*fig. 288*).

(2) Cut a piece of bump or domette interlining to these same measurements.

Fig. 287 *Wastepaper bins and tidies*

Fig. 288 *Taking the measurements of the bin*

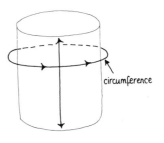

circumference

134

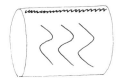

Fig. 289 *Applying adhesive to the bin*

Fig. 290 *Interlining applied and the raw edges butted together*

(3) Cut a piece of face fabric to these measurements but add 2.5 cm (1 in) to the circumference measurement for turnings. Make sure that the fabric is cut so that the selvedge runs from the top to the bottom of the bin.

(4) Turn the bin on its side to apply the interlining. Apply an even strip of adhesive vertically from the top to the bottom of the bin. Apply the interlining, making sure that the fabric is applied in a perfectly straight line at right angles to the top of the bin. (If there is a seam where the metal is joined, use it as a guide line to get a straight edge.)

(5) Apply the adhesive in a zigzag, spreading it as evenly as possible over the bin (*fig. 289*). Apply the bump or domette to it, stretching it slightly to obtain a smooth finish. Finish off by trimming the fabric if necessary, and butting the raw edges together (*fig. 290*).

(6) Apply the face fabric to the bin in the same way as the interlining but apply the adhesive to the interlining at the top and lower edges of the bin only. Finish by turning in a 1.3 cm (½ in) hem to make a neat join. Make sure that the fabric is firmly positioned and that the grain line is straight.

(7) Cover the raw edges at the top and bottom of the bin with braid, trimming or velvet ribbon. Do not apply braid down the seam line.

The face fabric looks attractive when embroidered or decorated with beads or appliqué before being applied to the bin, and this is a particularly interesting way of treating bins for children's rooms, playrooms or studies (*fig. 287*).

Shower Curtains

These are constructed in the same way as unlined curtains (Chapter 5) but they do not require as much fullness. Shower curtains are usually fixed by hooks and rings from a pole or decorative rod, or they can hang from a special ceiling-mounted curtain track (*figs. 291 and 292*).

Fig. 291 *Making a shower cubicle using ceiling mounted curtain track*

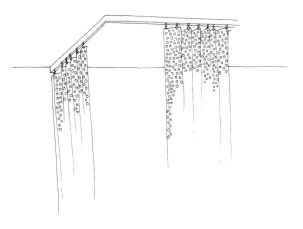

135

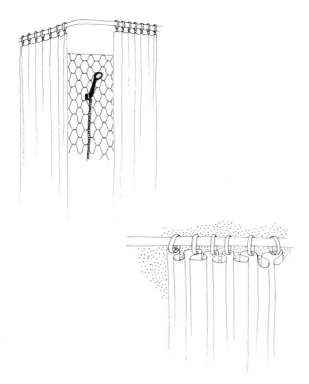

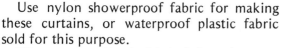

Fig. 292 *Shower curtain hanging from rings from a decorative rod*

Fig. 293 *Trimming towels to match other accessories*

Use nylon showerproof fabric for making these curtains, or waterproof plastic fabric sold for this purpose.

When sewing plastic fabric follow the same guidelines as when sewing p.v.c. (Chapter 10), i.e. use synthetic thread and a long loose stitch when machining, and French seams for joining widths or fabric together.

Choose a standard nylon heading tape for the curtain heading and hang the curtains from rings from the shower rail or decorative rod round the bath or shower.

Trimmings for Towels

Plain coloured towels can be successfully trimmed using pieces of fabric matching curtains, cushions, lampshades and other items. Alternatively, trim the ends of towels with hard-wearing coarse lace that washes well (*fig. 293*).

Fig. 294 *Applying the trimming to the towel*

(1) Cut four pieces of fabric 6.4–7.5 cm (2½–3 in) wide by the width of the towel plus 2.5 cm (1 in) for turnings.
(2) Turn in each piece 1.3 cm (½ in) all round and tack to each end of the towel on both sides. Machine stitch in position (*fig. 294*).

SUPPLIERS AND USEFUL ADDRESSES

U.K.

John Lewis
Oxford St
London, W.1., and branches:—

London
Jones Brothers   Peter Jones
Holloway.   Sloane Square.

John Lewis   Pratts
Brent Cross.   Streatham.

Outside London
Bainbridge   John Lewis
Newcastle-upon-Tyne.   Edinburgh.

Caleys   John Lewis
Windsor.   Milton Keynes.

Cole Bros.   Knight and Lee
Sheffield.   Southsea.

George Henry Lee   Robert Sayle
Liverpool.   Cambridge.

Heelas   Trewin Brothers
Reading.   Watford.

Jessops   Tyrrell and Green
Nottingham.   Southampton.

Furnishing fabrics; shower curtain fabric; roller blind kits and fabrics; patchwork templates; downproof cambric; heat-resistant table covering; poly-cotton sheeting.

Distinctive Trimmings
11 Marylebone Lane
London, W.1.

and

17 Church St,
London, W.8.
Trimmings for soft furnishings, and accessories.

The Upstairs Shop
22 Pimlico Rd
London, S.W.1.
01-730-7502
Fabrics. Bias binding dyed to match fabrics.

Just Gingham
44 Pimlico Rd
London S.W.1.
01-730-2588
Fabrics.

Laura Ashley
183 Sloane St
London, S.W.1. and branches
Co-ordinating fabrics and wallpapers.

C.V.P. Designs
5 Weighhouse St
Mayfair, London, W.1.
01-629-0900
Fabrics.

The Colefax and Fowler Chintz Shop
39 Brook St
Mayfair, London, W.1.

149 Ebury St
London S.W.1
Fabrics.

Osborne & Little
304 Kings Rd
London, S.W.3.
01-352-1456
Co-ordinating fabrics and wallpapers.

A. Sanderson & Son
Berners St
London, W.1.
Fabrics and wallpapers.

Limericks
110 Court Rd
Westcliffe-on-Sea, Essex.
Poly-cotton sheeting. Cotton damask, white linen, ticking, curtain lining, etc. Pillows (including continental size 68.5 x 68.5 cm, 27 x 27 in).

Descamps
197 Sloane St
London, S.W.1.
Fabrics for furnishing and bed linen.

McCullach & Wallis Ltd
25—26 New Bond St
London, W.1.
Haberdashery.

Habitat Shops
Roller blind kits and fabrics.

The Patchwork Dog and The Calico Cat
21 Chalk Farm Rd
London, N.W.1.
Synthetic wadding. Kapok. Patchwork templates.

Arrowtip Ltd
31—35 Stannary St
London, SE11 4AA.
01-735 8848
Expanded polystyrene beads.

Beckfoot Mill
Harden
Bingley, Yorkshire.
Fillings for cushions, toys, etc.

Russell Trading Co
75 Paradise St
Liverpool, L1 3BP
051-709-5752
Synthetic fillings, furnishing fabrics, etc.

The Felt & Hessian Shop
34 Greville St
London E.C.1.
01-405-6215
Felt and hessian in a wide range of colours.

Kirsch (Antiference) Ltd
Bicester Rd
Aylesbury, Bucks.
Tracks, fittings for curtains, bed canopies and drapes.

Graber-Marvic Textiles Ltd
41—42 Berners St
London, W1P 3AA.
Tracks and fittings for curtains. Fabrics and trimmings.

Rufflette Ltd
Sharston Rd
Wythenshawe
Manchester.
Tracks and fittings for curtains. Trimmings

David Hicks
Jermyn St
London, W.1.
Furnishing fabrics.

Culpepper
21 Bruton St
London, W.1.
Herbs and hops for filling cushions, etc.

Taylor of London
166 Sloane St
London, S.W.1.
Pot pourri, lavender and herbs for filling cushions, etc.

Woods of Windsor
Queen Charlotte St
Windsor.
Pot pourri, lavender for filling cushions, etc.

Paperchase
Tottenham Court Rd
London, W.1.
Stencils, acetate film.

Dylon International Ltd
London, SE26 5HD.
Fabric paints and dyes.

Arts and Crafts Unlimited
49 Shelton St
London, W.C.2.
Fabric dyes.

A.M. Row & Son Ltd
42 Market Place
Ripon, Yorkshire.
Patchwork templates.

Dryad Handicrafts
Northgates
Leicester.
Art and craft materials.

Nottingham Handicrafts Co
Melton Rd
West Bridgford
Nottingham, NG2 6HD.
Trimmings, etc.

Fred Aldous Ltd
The Handicraft Centre
P.O. Box 135, 37 Lever St
Manchester, M50 1UX.
Trimmings, etc.

Lewis & Wayne
13 Elystan St
London, S.W.3.
and
9 Streatham High Rd
London, S.W.16.
Specialist cleaners for curtains and soft furn-ishings.

Pilgrim Payne & Co
Park St. Works
Latimer Place
London, W.10.
Specialist cleaners for curtains and soft furn-ishings.

Pallu and Lake
18 Newman St
London W.1

U.S.A.

American Handicrafts
2617 W Seventh St
Fort Worth, Texas 76707.

Economy Handicrafts
50–21 69th St
Woodside, New York 11377.

Lee Wards
Elgin
Illinois 60120.

Peters Valley Craftsmen
Layton, New Jersey 07851.

Chain stores:—
    Ben Franklin Stores
    Jefferson Stores
    Kay Mart
    M.H. Lamston
    The May Co
    Neisners
    J.C. Penney Stores
    Sears Roebuck
    Two Guys
    Woolworths

Kirsch Co
Sturgis
MI 49091

GLOSSARY

British terms and their American counterparts

appliqué—pieces of fabric or felt applied to another fabric

broderie anglaise—cotton or cotton/polyester fabric with cut-out embroidery designs

buckram—coarse fabric used for stiffening curtain headings

bump—coarse fabric or matting

calico—unbleached muslin

cambric—closely woven, polished cotton used to enclose feathers or down

crossway strip—bias strip—a strip of fabric cut accros the weft and the warp of the fabric

cushions—all decorative pillows other than bed pillows

domette—baize or coarse flannel in which the warp is cotton and the filling woollen

duvet—bed covering used in Northern Europe that takes the place of both top sheet and blanket

felt—a non-woven fabric that does not fray

heading—top edge of a curtain from which the curtain is hung

lining sateen—closely woven cotton fabric with a shiny surface used for lining curtains

loose cover—slip cover

metre stick—yardstick

pelmet—fixture at the head of the curtains that conceals the tracks and fittings

repp—transversely corded or ribbed fabric

roller blinds—window shades

selvedge—the edges of a woven fabric running parallel to the warp

squab—a loose cushion which is tied to a stool or a chair seat

tacking cotton—basting thread

template—a pattern used as a guide when cutting out

turnings—seam allowance

valance—pleated or gathered piece of fabric used at the top of a curtain. Can also be used to describe fabric fitted under the mattress to conceal the base of the bed

Velcro—a touch-and-close fastening for cushions, pelmets, etc. One side of the tape is covered with a nylon fuzz and the other with tiny nylon hooks which catch on to the fuzz when the two surfaces are pressed together

Vilene—bonded fabric used for interfacing

wadding—batting or filling

window treatments—window furnishings

zipper foot—a half foot which is attached to the sewing machine to facilitate stitching close to the zipper or piping. The design of the foot varies with the make of machine

BIBLIOGRAPHY

Patchwork, Averil Colby, Batsford, London, 1978; Branford, Boston, 1976

Quilting, Averil Colby, Batsford, London, 1976; Scribner, New York, 1972

The Batsford Book of Soft Furnishings, Angela Fishburn, Batsford, London, 1978; Larousse, New York, 1978

Lampshades: Technique and Design, Angela Fishburn, Batsford, London, 1975; Drake, New York, 1977

Decoration with Fabrics, David Hicks, Weidenfeld & Nicolson, 1971

Living with Design, David Hicks, Weidenfeld & Nicolson, 1979

Inspiration for Embroidery, Constance Howard, Batsford, London, 1976

The Batsford Book of Sewing, Ann Ladbury, Batsford, 1978

Modern Upholstering Techniques, Robert J. McDonald, Batsford, 1981

Textiles: Properties and Behaviour, Edward Miller, Batsford, 1973

Quilting: Technique, Design and Application, Eirian Short, Batsford, 1981

Colour, Mitchell Beazley, 1980

Also useful is *The Textile Care Labelling Code*, British Standards Institution, BSI Sales Branch, 101 Pentonville Road, London N1 9ND

Metric Conversion Table

in.	cm.	in.	cm.	in.	cm.
$\frac{1}{8}$	0.3	8	20.5	22	56.0
¼	0.6	8½	21.5	23	58.5
½	1.3	9	23.0	24	61.0
$\frac{3}{8}$	1.0	9½	24.0	25	63.5
¾	1.9	10	25.5	26	66.0
1	2.5	10½	26.5	27	68.5
1¼	3.2	11	28.0	28	71.0
1½	3.8	11½	29.0	29	73.5
2	5.0	12	30.5	30	76.0
2½	6.4	12½	31.5	31	78.5
		13	33.0	32	81.5
3	7.5	13½	34.5	33	84.0
3½	9.0	14	35.5	34	86.5
4	10.0	14½	37.0	35	89.0
4½	11.5	15	38.0	36	91.5
5	12.5	16	40.5	37	94.0
5½	14.0	17	43.0	38	96.5
6	15.0	18	45.5	39	99.0
6½	16.5	19	48.5	40	101.5
7	18.0	20	51.0	48	122.0
7½	19.0	21	53.5	54	137.0

INDEX